I0427688

PREFACE

1. Scope

This publication is the keystone document of the joint logistics series. It provides overarching joint doctrine on logistic support to joint operations. It provides commanders and staff guidance and considerations for planning, execution, and assessment of joint operations. It also discusses responsibilities, authorities, and control options available to a joint force commander (JFC) and provides precepts to influence the commander's decision-making process.

2. Purpose

This publication has been prepared under the direction of the Chairman of the Joint Chiefs of Staff (CJCS). It sets forth joint doctrine for the activities and performance of the Armed Forces of the United States in joint operations and provides the doctrinal basis for the conduct of joint logistics. It provides military guidance for the exercise of authority by combatant commanders and JFCs. It prescribes the doctrinal framework within which logistics can be optimized for operations, education, and training. This publication is intended to provide guidance to JFCs and staffs, their subordinate component commands, and combat support agencies (CSAs) for joint logistics operations including the incorporation of interagency and multinational elements. It is not the intent of this publication to restrict the authority of the JFC from organizing the force and executing the mission in a manner the JFC deems most appropriate to ensure unity of effort in the accomplishment of the overall objective.

3. Application

a. Joint doctrine established in this publication applies to the Joint Staff, commanders of combatant commands, subunified commands, joint task forces, subordinate components of these commands, the Services, and CSAs.

b. The guidance in this publication is authoritative; as such, this doctrine will be followed except when, in the judgment of the commander, exceptional circumstances dictate otherwise. If conflicts arise between the contents of this publication and the contents of Service publications, this publication will take precedence unless the CJCS, normally in coordination with the other members of the Joint Chiefs of Staff, has provided more current and specific guidance. Commanders of forces operating as part of a multinational (alliance or coalition) military command should follow multinational doctrine and procedures ratified by the United States. For doctrine and procedures not ratified by the United States, commanders should evaluate and follow the multinational command's doctrine and procedures, where applicable and be consistent with US law, regulations, and doctrine.

For the Chairman of the Joint Chiefs of Staff:

DAVID L. GOLDFEIN, Lt Gen, USAF
Director, Joint Staff

SUMMARY OF CHANGES
REVISION OF JOINT PUBLICATION 4-0
DATED 18 JULY 2008

- **Adds Chapter III, "Coordinating and Synchronizing Joint Logistics."**

- **Introduces the term "joint logistics enterprise (JLEnt)."**

- **Introduces the Joint Staff, J-3 as the joint deployment process owner.**

- **Introduces the term "JLEnt visibility."**

- **Includes the term "common-user logistics" from Joint Publication (JP) 4-07,** *Joint Tactics, Techniques, and Procedures for Common-User Logistics During Joint Operations,* **and cancels JP 4-07.**

- **Revises the use of logistic functions and subordinate capabilities.**

- **Introduces health services and subordinate capabilities: health service delivery, force health protection, and health system support.**

- **Replaces "base camp services" with "contingency base services."**

- **Introduces the term "base operating support integrator."**

- **Discusses base and installation support.**

- **Revises the joint deployment and distribution operations center's responsibility.**

- **Revises the Defense Logistics Agency's role.**

- **Introduces geographic combatant commander (GCC) option selection and design.**

- **Introduces the term "operational energy."**

- **Revises Chapter IV, "Joint Logistics Planning," to improve continuity with JP 5-0,** *Joint Operation Planning,* **and JP 3-0,** *Joint Operations,* **to address Department of Defense transition to Adaptive Planning and Execution System.**

- **Revises Chapter IV, "Joint Logistics Planning," to codify logistics planning process segments within and across the joint operation planning process.**

- Revises Chapter IV, "Joint Logistics Planning," to identify and address planning process actions and key information sets to facilitate joint development of global or theater campaign plans, subordinate campaign plans, and contingency plans tasked in the Joint Strategic Capabilities Plan or as directed by the combatant commander.

- Revises Chapter IV, "Joint Logistics Planning," to integrate, synchronize, and prioritize joint logistics capabilities toward achieving the supported commander's operational objectives and desired outcome during all phases of plan development.

- Revises Chapter IV, "Joint Logistics Planning," to codify the logistics, logistics capabilities, and logistics estimate as part of the Secretary of Defense plans in-progress review process.

- Deletes Chapter V, "Controlling Logistics."

- Adds an appendix on theater logistics overview.

- Adds an appendix on logistics staff estimate format.

- Revises an appendix on joint logistics staff organizations.

- Revises an appendix on executive agents.

- Adds an appendix on GCC logistics control option selection and design descriptions.

- Revises the definition of "concept of logistic support."

- Adds the term "lead Service or agency for common-user logistics."

- Deletes the definition for "support items."

- Deletes the definition for "time-definite delivery."

TABLE OF CONTENTS

CHAPTER V
EXECUTING JOINT LOGISTICS

APPENDIX

GLOSSARY

FIGURE

Intentionally Blank

EXECUTIVE SUMMARY
COMMANDER'S OVERVIEW

- **Provides an overview of joint logistics.**

- **Describes the core logistics functions.**

- **Covers coordinating and synchronizing joint logistics.**

- **Explains joint logistics planning and execution.**

Joint Logistics Overview

Joint logistics is the coordinated use, synchronization, and sharing of two or more Military Departments' logistic resources to support the joint force.

The relative combat power that military forces can generate against an adversary is constrained by a nation's capability to plan for, gain access to, and deliver forces and materiel to required points of application. The joint logistics enterprise (JLEnt) projects and sustains a logistically ready joint force by leveraging Department of Defense (DOD), interagency, nongovernmental agencies, multinational, and industrial resources. The identification of established coordination frameworks, agreements, and other connections creates an efficient and effective logistic network to support the mission.

Joint Logistics Environment

Operations are distributed and conducted rapidly and simultaneously across multiple joint operations areas (JOAs), within a single theater, or across boundaries of more than one geographic combatant commander (GCC). These operations can involve a variety of military forces, other governmental organizations, and multinational forces. The joint logistics environment is the sum of conditions and circumstances that affect logistics.

Key Organizations

The key DOD organizations in the JLEnt include the Services, combatant commands (CCMDs), Defense Logistics Agency (DLA), United States Transportation Command (USTRANSCOM), the Joint Staff J-3 [Operations Directorate], and the Joint Staff J-4 [Logistics Directorate].

The **Services** are responsible for operational logistics support systems, platforms, and their execution to support the force. They are responsible to maintain systems' life-cycle readiness.

DLA is the DOD executive agent (EA) for subsistence, bulk fuel, construction and barrier materiel, and medical material. DLA also manages a global network of distribution depots that receives, stores, and issues a wide range of commodities owned by the Services, General Services Administration, and DLA.

USTRANSCOM is responsible for providing air, land, and sea transportation, terminal management, and aerial refueling to support the global deployment, employment, sustainment, and redeployment of US forces.

As the joint deployment process owner, the **Joint Staff J-3** is responsible for leading the collaborative efforts of the joint planning and execution community to improve the joint deployment and redeployment processes.

The **Joint Staff J-4** leads the DOD efforts in the JLEnt and assesses the preparedness of the DOD global logistics force.

Joint Logistics Imperatives

Joint logistics focuses on three imperatives to influence mission success: unity of effort, JLEnt visibility, and rapid and precise response. These imperatives define the desired attributes of a federation of systems, processes, and organizations that effectively adapt within a constantly changing operational environment to meet the emerging needs of the supported joint force commander (JFC).

Logistics Integration

Commanders and staffs apply basic principles, control resources, and manage capabilities to provide sustained joint logistics. Logisticians can use the principles of logistics as a guideline to assess how effective logistics are integrated into plans and execution. To achieve full integration, commanders and their logisticians coordinate, synchronize, plan, execute, and assess logistic support to joint forces during all phases of the operation.

Core Logistics Functions

Introduction

The core logistic functions are: deployment and distribution, supply, maintenance, logistic services, operational contract support (OCS), engineering, and health services (HS). The core logistic functions are considered during the employment of US military forces in coordinated action toward a common objective and provide global force projection and sustainment.

Deployment and Distribution	The global dispersion of the threats, coupled with the necessity to rapidly deploy, execute, and sustain operations worldwide, makes the deployment and distribution capability the cornerstone of joint logistics. These operational factors necessitate a shift from a supply-based system to a system that is primarily distribution-based with beginning-to-end synchronization to meet JFC requirements.
Supply	DLA is primarily responsible for DOD supply chain operations and manages the supply process to provide common commodities and services to joint forces. Planning for supply operations requires a collaborative environment to fully consider all major components of the JLEnt to include the return and retrograde of equipment and supplies.
Maintenance	Maintenance supports system readiness for the JFC. The Services, as part of their Title 10, United States Code (USC), responsibilities, execute maintenance as a core logistics function. The Services employ a maintenance strategy of depot and field level maintenance to improve the JFC's freedom of action and sustain the readiness and capabilities of assigned units.
Logistic Services	Logistic services comprise the support capabilities that collectively enable the US to rapidly provide global sustainment for our military forces. Logistic services include many highly scalable and disparate capabilities. Included in this area are food service, water and ice service, contingency base services, hygiene services, and mortuary affairs.
Operational Contract Support	OCS provides the combatant commander (CCDR) the tools and processes to manage the variety of services that may be required, such as base operational support, transportation, and security. Within OCS are contract support integration and contractor management.
Engineering	Joint force engineers provide comprehensive recommendations to the commander on all engineering capabilities. They provide the ability to execute and integrate combat, general, and geospatial engineering to meet national and JFC requirements to assure mobility, provide infrastructure to position, project, protect, and sustain the joint force.

Health Services

The purpose of HS is to improve the health readiness of individual personnel as well as the overall force and provide HS in order to ensure mission accomplishment. HS includes all services performed, provided, or arranged that promote, improve, conserve, or restore the mental and physical wellbeing of personnel.

Coordinating and Synchronizing Joint Logistics

Logistics Authorities

Directive Authority for Logistics (DAFL). CCDRs exercise authoritative direction over logistics, in accordance with Title 10, USC, Section 164. DAFL cannot be delegated or transferred. However, the CCDR may delegate the responsibility for the planning, execution, and/or management of common support capabilities to a subordinate JFC or Service component commander to accomplish the subordinate JFC's or Service component commander's mission. For some commodities or support services common to two or more Services, the Secretary of Defense (SecDef) or the Deputy Secretary of Defense may designate one provider as the EA.

Lead Service. The CCDR may choose to assign specific common user logistics functions, to include both planning and execution to a lead Service. These assignments can be for single or multiple common logistics functions, and may also be based on phases or locations within the area of responsibility (AOR).

Base Operating Support-Integrator (BOS-I). When multiple Service components share a common base of operations, the JFC may choose to designate a single Service component or joint task force as the BOS-I for the location. The BOS-I facilitates unity of effort by coordinating sustainment operations at the location.

Joint Logistics Roles and Responsibilities

The **Assistant Secretary of Defense for Logistics and Materiel Readiness** is the principal advisor to the Under Secretary of Defense for Acquisition, Technology, and Logistics (USD[AT&L]), SecDef, and Deputy Secretary of Defense on logistics and materiel readiness in the DOD and is the principal logistics official within senior management.

The **Military Departments** authorities include recruiting, organizing, supplying, equipping, training, servicing, mobilizing, demobilizing, administering, and maintaining forces; constructing, outfitting, and repairing military equipment; constructing, maintaining, and repairing buildings, structures, and utilities; and acquiring, managing, and disposing of real property or natural resources.

The **[Service] components** provide logistics support for Service and all forces assigned to joint commands, including procurement, distribution, supply, equipment, and maintenance, unless otherwise directed by SecDef.

CCDRs are responsible for the coordination and approval of the aspects of administration, support (including control of resources and equipment, internal organization, and training) and discipline necessary to carry out missions assigned to the command.

Combat support agencies (CSAs) perform support functions or provide supporting operational capabilities, consistent with their establishing directives and pertinent DOD planning guidance. The USD(AT&L) is the principal staff assistant for DLA, the Defense Contract Management Agency, and the Defense Threat Reduction Agency.

Combatant Commander's Logistics Directorate

The logistics directorate of a joint staff (J-4) at the CCMD is responsible for logistics planning and execution in support of joint operations. They perform this function by integrating, coordinating, and synchronizing Service component and CSA logistics capabilities to support the joint force. The J-4 staff supports the operations directorate of a joint staff in the planning and executing of requirements for the joint reception, staging, onward movement, and integration process as well as contingency base planning and sustainment. The J-4 establishes a joint logistics operations center (JLOC) to monitor and control the execution of logistics in support of on-going operations. At time of need a supported GCC can create a joint deployment and distribution operations center (JDDOC) and incorporate its capabilities into the staff functions. The JDDOC develops deployment and distribution plans, integrates multinational and/or interagency deployment and distribution, and coordinates and synchronizes supply, transportation, and related distribution activities. The CCDR may also establish boards, centers, offices, and cells (e.g., subarea petroleum office, joint facilities utilization board, joint mortuary affairs office) to meet increased requirements and to coordinate the logistics effort.

Logistics Control Options

The CCDR may elect to control logistics through the J-4 staff. The CCDR may elect to assign responsibility to establish a joint command for logistics to a subordinate Service component. When exercising this option, the CCDR retains DAFL, and must specify the control and tasking authorities being bestowed upon the subordinate joint command for logistics, as well as the command relationships it will have with the Service components. Planners should consider areas where common-user logistics organizational options are best suited.

Joint Logistics Planning

Joint logistics planning is conducted under the construct of joint operation planning.

Joint logistics planning provides the process and the means to integrate, synchronize, and prioritize joint logistics capabilities toward achieving the supported commander's operational objectives and desired outcome during all phases of plan development.

Planning Functions

Joint operation planning encompasses a number of elements, including four planning functions: strategic guidance, concept development, plan development, and plan assessment. Depending upon the type of planning and time available, these functions can be sequential or concurrent.

Joint Operation Planning Process

Joint operation planning is the overarching process that guides CCDRs in developing plans for the employment of military power within the context of national strategic objectives and national military strategy to shape events, meet contingencies, and respond to unforeseen crises. Logistics input is derived from mission analysis, course of action (COA) development, analysis, selection, and plan development to include preparation and submission of logistics supportability analysis.

Theater Logistics Analysis

The theater logistics analysis (TLA) is a supporting process facilitating development of the theater logistics overview (TLO) through examination, assessment, and codification of an understanding of current conditions of the operational environment. The TLA provides a rough detailed country by country analysis of key infrastructure by location or installation (main operating base/forward operating site/cooperative security location); footprint projections; and host nation (HN) agreements required to support logistically theater peacetime through contingency operations.

Theater Logistics Overview

Development of the TLO is a segment of the iterative planning process which addresses identification, understanding, and framing the theater's overarching mission at the campaign level and uses the TLA combined with elements of operational art to conceive and construct a logistics support approach identified for theater phase 0 to phase V operations.

Logistics Estimate

The logistics estimate is an analysis of how combat service support factors can affect mission accomplishment. It contains the logistics staff's comparison of requirements and capabilities, conclusions, and recommendations about the feasibility of supporting a specified COA. This estimate includes how the core logistics functions affect various COA(s).

Concept of Logistic Support

The concept of logistic support (COLS) establishes priorities of support across all phases of operations to support the JFC's concept of operations. A COLS addresses the sustainment of forces to include identification and status of theater support bases, intermediate staging bases, forward staging bases, and assignment of contingency base operation responsibilities.

Executing Joint Logistics

Joint Logistics Execution

JFCs adapt to evolving mission requirements and operate effectively across a range of military operations. These operations differ in complexity and duration. The joint logistician must be aware of the characteristics and focus of these operations and tailor logistics support appropriately.

Essential Elements for Joint Logistics Execution

The CCMD J-4 is responsible for an effective transition of logistics operations from peacetime or planning activities to monitoring, assessing, planning, and directing logistics operations throughout the theater. This transition may occur through the directed expansion of the JLOC and/or the CCDR's JDDOC. A role of the joint logistician is to support the JFC in achieving situational awareness in order to make decisions and disseminate and execute directives. Maintaining situational awareness requires maintaining visibility over the status and location of resources, over the current and future requirements of the force, and over the joint and component processes that deliver support to the joint force. In order to provide this visibility, timely and accurate data and information are required for all equipment, sustaining supplies, repair parts, munitions, fuel and etc., moving into, within, exiting, being stored, or stored in the GCC's AOR.

Terminating Joint Operations

When it has been determined that joint operations should be terminated, joint logistic operations focus tasks that include redeploying personnel and materiel from the JOA to a new operational area or home station/demobilization station; transitioning materiel to HN; foreign military sales; or disposal of materiel.

CONCLUSION

This publication is the keystone document of the joint logistics series. It provides overarching joint doctrine on logistic support to joint operations. It provides commanders and staff guidance and considerations for planning, execution, and assessment of joint operations. It also discusses responsibilities, authorities, and control options available to a JFC and provides precepts to influence the commander's decision-making process.

CHAPTER I
JOINT LOGISTICS OVERVIEW

> *"Logistics is the bridge between the economy of the Nation and the tactical operations of its combat forces. Obviously then, the logistics system must be in harmony, both with the economic system of the Nation and with the tactical concepts and environment of the combat forces."*
>
> **Rear Admiral Henry E. Eccles, US Navy (1959)**

1. Introduction

a. Sustainment is one of the six joint functions (command and control [C2], intelligence, fires, movement and maneuver, protection, and sustainment) described in Joint Publication (JP) 3-0, *Joint Operations.* Sustainment provides the joint force commanders (JFCs) freedom of action, endurance, and the ability to extend operational reach. Effective sustainment determines the depth to which the joint force can conduct decisive operations, allowing the JFC to seize, retain, and exploit the initiative. Sustainment is primarily the responsibility of the supported combatant commander (CCDR) and subordinate Service component commanders in close cooperation with the Services, combat support agencies (CSAs), and supporting commands. Sustainment is the provision of logistics and personnel services necessary to maintain and prolong operations until mission accomplishment and redeployment of the force. Joint logistics supports sustained readiness for joint forces.

b. JP 4-0, *Joint Logistics,* focuses on logistics. This publication provides logistics guidance essential to the operational capability and success of the joint force. JP 4-0, *Joint Logistics,* also provides a framework for CCDRs and subordinate JFCs to integrate capabilities from national, multinational, Services, and CSAs to provide forces properly equipped and trained, when and where required.

c. Future operations will take place in an increasingly contested global forum, in non-permissive, uncertain, and hostile environments, confronted by physical, cyberspace, and diplomatic restrictions. To meet the wide variety of global challenges, CCDRs, JFCs, and their staffs must develop a clear understanding of joint logistics to include the relationship between logistical organizations, personnel, core functions, principles, imperatives, and the operational environment. A diverse and rapidly changing operational environment with increased threats to logistics requires JFCs to deploy strong, agile, and capable military forces whose actions are synchronized with other instruments of US national power and partner nations (PNs). This publication provides guidance for joint logistics, describes core logistic functions essential to success, and offers a framework to plan, execute, assess, and coordinate joint logistics.

d. Logistics concerns the integration of strategic, operational, and tactical support efforts within the theater, while scheduling the mobilization and movement of forces and materiel to support the JFC's concept of operations (CONOPS). The relative combat power that military forces can generate against an adversary is constrained by a nation's capability to plan for, gain access to, and deliver forces and materiel to required points of application.

The core logistics functions are: supply, maintenance, deployment and distribution, health services (HS), logistic services, engineering, and operational contract support (OCS) (discussed in Chapter II, "Core Logistics Functions"). Logistics includes planning and executing the movement and support of forces as well as those aspects of military operations that deal with:

(1) Materiel acquisition, receipt, storage, movement, distribution, maintenance, evacuation, and disposition.

(2) Patient movement (PM), evacuation, and hospitalization.

(3) Facilities and infrastructure acquisition, construction, maintenance, operation, and disposition.

(4) Logistic services (food, water and ice, contingency basing and hygiene).

(5) OCS (synchronization of contract support for operations and contract management).

(6) Infrastructure assessment, repairs, and maintenance.

(7) Common-user logistics (CUL) support to other US Government departments and agencies, intergovernmental organizations (IGOs), nongovernmental organizations (NGOs), and other nations.

(8) Detention compounds (establish and sustain large-scale to support enduring detainee operations).

(9) Host-nation support.

(10) Disposal operations.

(11) In-transit visibility (ITV) and asset visibility (AV).

(12) Engineering support.

2. Joint Logistics

a. Joint logistics is the coordinated use, synchronization, and sharing of two or more Military Departments' logistics resources to support the joint force. The joint logistics enterprise (JLEnt) projects and sustains a logistically ready joint force by leveraging Department of Defense (DOD), interagency, nongovernmental agencies, multinational, and industrial resources. The identification of established coordination frameworks, agreements, and other connections creates an efficient and effective logistic network to support the mission.

b. **JLEnt.** The JLEnt is a multitiered matrix of key global logistics providers cooperatively structured to achieve a common purpose. It may be bound by an assortment of collaborative agreements, contracts, policy, legislation, or treaties designed to make it function in the best interest of the JFC or other supported organization. The JLEnt includes organizations and partnerships from the Services, combatant commands (CCMDs), joint task forces (JTFs), CSAs, other US Government departments and agencies, and NGOs. Commercial partners also play a vital role in virtually all aspects of the JLEnt and function on a global scale providing comprehensive, end-to-end capabilities. The JLEnt may also include multinational partners. Participants operate across the strategic, operational, and tactical levels—many are affiliated with either supported or supporting commands and operate under a variety of command relationships. Knowing the roles, responsibilities, and authorities of JLEnt partners is essential to planning, executing, controlling, and assessing logistic operations. JLEnt partners must collaborate to ensure the coordinated employment and sharing of capabilities and resources.

    c. **Building Partnership Capacity (BPC).** Complicated supply lines, finite resources, the challenges of providing robust logistics in austere environments, and shared lines of communications (LOCs) require the ability to establish and foster nontraditional partnerships. BPC is important for sharing the costs and responsibilities, improving information flow, and establishing PN agreements. BPC includes coordination of resources with multinational partners, IGOs, and NGOs. BPC improves unity of effort within the entire JLEnt. BPC is an essential component of joint operations because the Services seldom have sufficient capability to support a joint force independently. BPC is an ongoing, long-term relationship development process that may not yield immediate results. The earlier the BPC efforts begin the better the chance of success for securing partner logistics support when needed. By combining capabilities, commanders can provide maximum effectiveness and flexibility to the joint force focused on common outcomes, that deliver sustained logistics support.

    d. **Personnel.** Joint logisticians are military personnel, civilians, and contractors who specialize in providing joint logistics support extending from the national industrial base to the end user. Joint logisticians plan, supervise, execute, synchronize, and coordinate core joint logistic functions. They understand tactical, operational, and strategic operations and synchronize efforts to effectively meet joint force requirements. Joint logisticians reach a level of proficiency through a combination of training, education, and operational experience created by Service, joint, and multinational duty assignments. Joint logisticians are exposed to logistic operations in a complex, diverse, and globally dispersed environment. Key attributes of a joint logistician include the ability to:

    (1) Apply policy and doctrine to improve joint force readiness.

    (2) Plan logistics support and integrate the support into the CCDR's plan.

    (3) Assist commanders in defining requirements and translating the commander's intent into logistics-related tasks.

    (4) Assess the operational situation to determine if joint logistic processes are established and working.

(5) Plan and execute joint logistics in a changing and uncertain environment.

(6) Forecast and articulate logistic requirements, shortfalls, risks, and supportability of operation plans (OPLANs).

(7) Coordinate Service, CSA, interagency, and multinational logistic capabilities.

(8) Assist JFCs as they exercise authority and provide direction for the common support of forces.

(9) Leverage commercial logistics best practices and processes.

(10) Identify risks that must be assumed and actions required to mitigate those risks.

3. Joint Logistics Environment

a. Military leaders conduct operations in a complicated, interconnected, and global environment. Operations are distributed and conducted rapidly and simultaneously across multiple joint operations areas (JOAs), within a single theater, or across boundaries of more than one geographic combatant commander (GCC). These operations can involve a variety of military forces, other governmental organizations, and multinational forces. The joint logistics environment is the sum of conditions and circumstances that affect logistics. The joint logistics environment exists at the strategic, operational, and tactical levels (see Figure I-1). Globalization, technology advancements, anti-access/area-denial, and flexible adversaries create a complex, ever-changing operational environment. Understanding this environment is essential to planning, executing, synchronizing, and coordinating logistic operations.

b. Joint logistics takes place throughout the operational environment. Service components and CSAs provide the expertise while the JFC's staff focuses on integrating the capabilities with operations. Access to secure networks is necessary to sustain joint force readiness and is achieved through Internet-based applications. Effective networks: find and access relevant information; facilitate collaboration; distribute data to forward deployed areas; increase performance and reliability; utilize the enterprise infrastructure for evolving DOD systems are resilient; and leverage PNs' capabilities.

4. Key Organizations

The JLEnt is connected by a web of relationships among global logistics providers, supporting and supported organizations and units, and other entities. The key DOD organizations in the JLEnt include the Services, CCMDs, Defense Logistics Agency (DLA), United States Transportation Command (USTRANSCOM), the Joint Staff J-3 [Operations Directorate], and the Joint Staff J-4 [Logistics Directorate] (see Figure I-2). Effective joint logistics depends on clearly defined roles, responsibilities, and relationships between the global logistics providers. Global logistics providers manage end-to-end processes that provide capabilities to the supported CCDR to fulfill requirements.

Joint Logistics Environment Operating Framework

Strategic Level	Operational Level	Tactical Level
Campaign Quality	Coordinate, Integrate, and Synchronize	Effectiveness
• Industrial base capacity enables sustained operations • End-to-end processes drive efficiencies across Services, agencies, and industry • Effectiveness dependent upon optimizing processes against required outcomes	• Combatant commander integrates joint requirements with national systems • Must optimize component, agency, and other partner nation capabilities to meet requirements • Most significant impact for joint logistics and the joint force	• Outcome is measured • Operational readiness enables "freedom of action" • Desired outcomes should drive optimization–from strategic to tactical

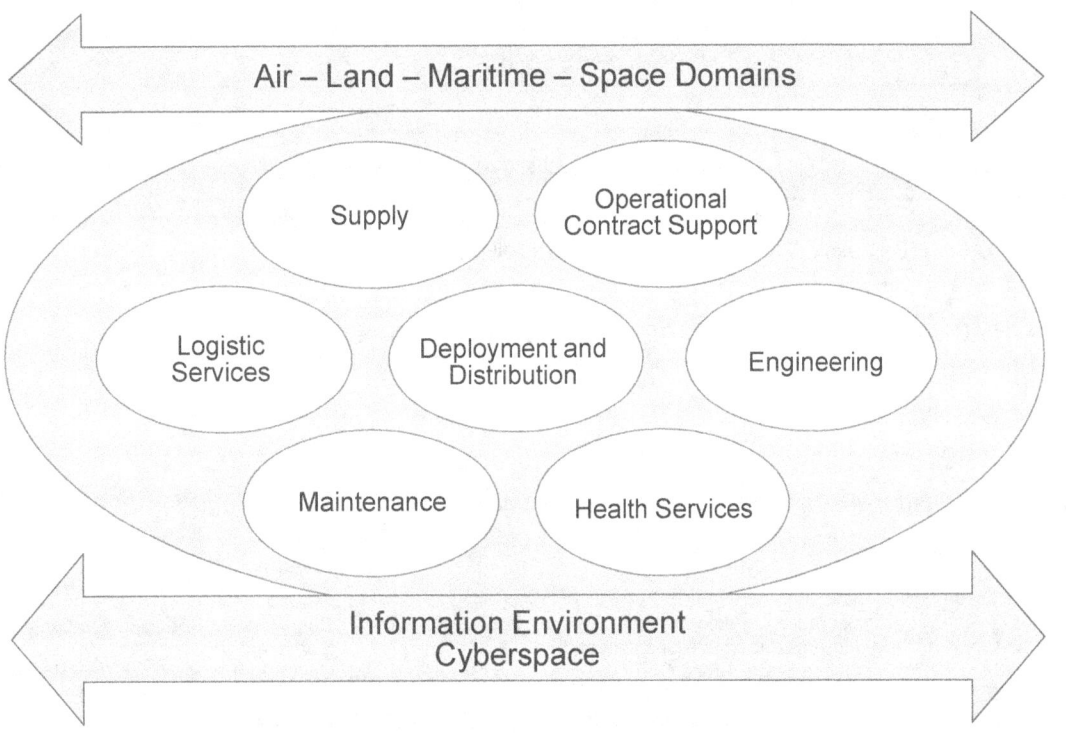

Air – Land – Maritime – Space Domains

Supply

Operational Contract Support

Logistic Services

Deployment and Distribution

Engineering

Maintenance

Health Services

Information Environment Cyberspace

Figure I-1. Joint Logistics Environment Operating Framework

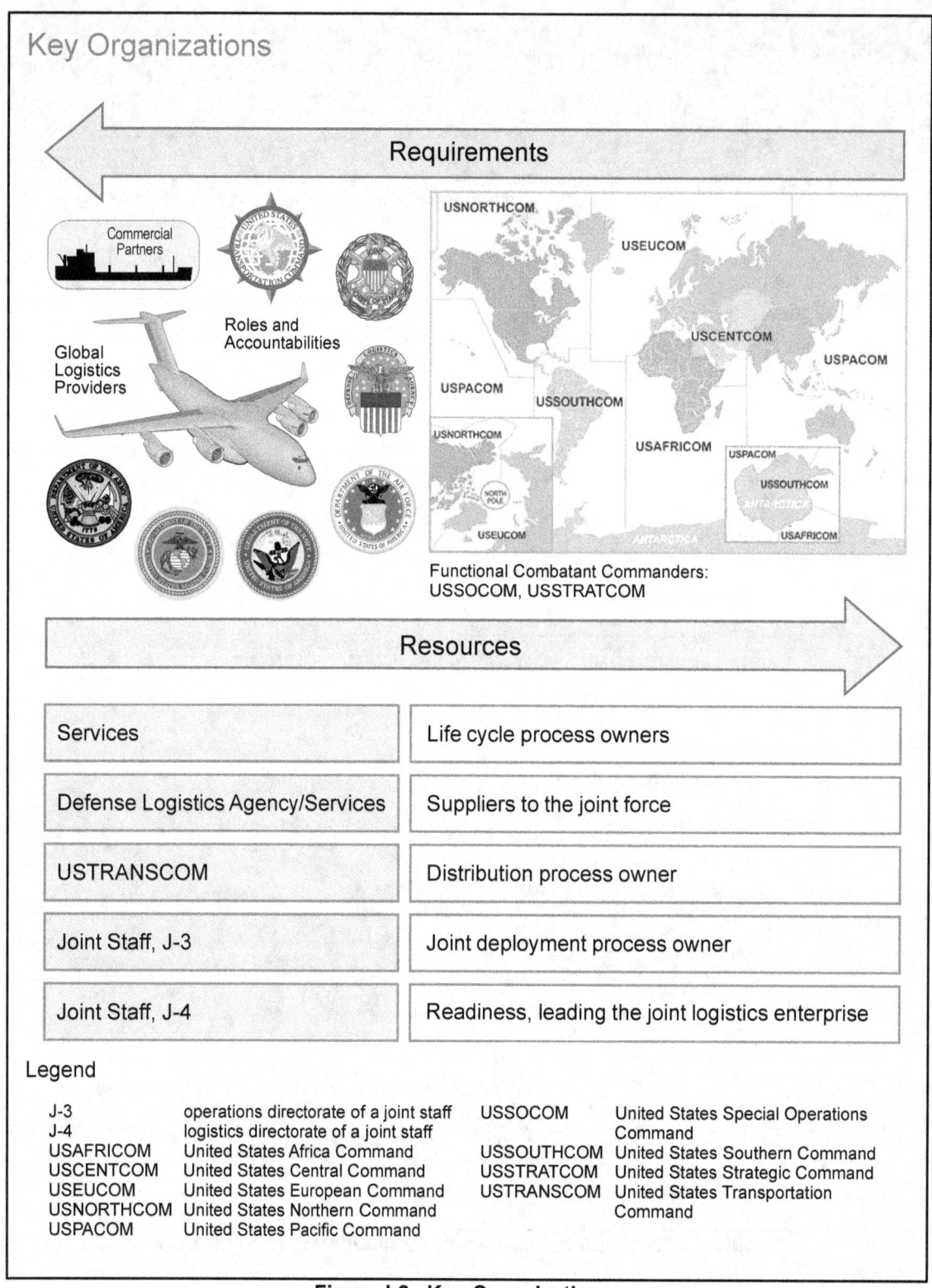

Figure I-2. Key Organizations

a. **Services.** In accordance with Title 10, United States Code (USC), the Services are responsible to prepare for employment of Service forces. They recruit, supply, organize, train, equip, service, mobilize, demobilize, provide administrative support, and maintain ready forces. Services are the center of a collaborative network, and their logistics organizations form the foundation of the JLEnt. The Services are responsible for operational logistics support systems, platforms, and their execution to support the force. They are responsible to maintain systems' life-cycle readiness.

b. **DLA.** DLA is the DOD executive agent (EA) for subsistence, bulk fuel, construction and barrier materiel, and medical material. DLA provides spares and reparables for weapons systems. DLA also manages a global network of distribution depots that receives, stores, and issues a wide range of commodities owned by the Services, General Services Administration, and DLA. Reutilization of end items and repair parts and disposing of hazardous property and waste is another major capability DLA executes for DOD. DLA is an integral part of the collaborative logistics network.

c. **USTRANSCOM.** USTRANSCOM is responsible for providing air, land, and sea transportation, terminal management, and aerial refueling to support the global deployment, employment, sustainment, and redeployment of US forces. USTRANSCOM serves as DOD's Mobility Joint Force Provider, DOD's Single Manager for Defense Transportation, and DOD's Single Manager for Patient Movement. USTRANSCOM is also responsible for synchronizing distribution planning for global operations in coordination with other CCMDs, Services, and agencies as directed. Additionally, USTRANSCOM serves as DOD's distribution process owner (DPO) responsible for coordinating and overseeing the DOD distribution system to provide interoperability, synchronization, and alignment of DOD-wide end-to-end distribution. Finally, USTRANSCOM is the force provider for joint enabling capabilities, a DOD resource that provides a JFC with the ability or functional means to plan and execute joint operations.

d. **The Joint Staff J-3.** The Joint Staff J-3 serves as the DOD joint deployment process owner (JDPO) and is responsible for maintaining the global capability for rapid and decisive military force power projection. As the JDPO, the Joint Staff J-3 is responsible for leading the collaborative efforts of the joint planning and execution community to improve the joint deployment and redeployment processes, while maintaining the overall effectiveness of these processes so that all supported JFCs and supporting DOD components can execute military force power projection more effectively and efficiently. The Joint Staff J-3 also serves as the primary joint force provider.

e. **The Joint Staff J-4.** The Joint Staff J-4 leads the DOD efforts in the JLEnt and assesses the preparedness of the DOD global logistics force.

5. **Joint Logistics Imperatives**

Joint logistics focuses on three imperatives to influence mission success: unity of effort, JLEnt visibility, and rapid and precise response. These imperatives define the desired attributes of a federation of systems, processes, and organizations that effectively adapt within a constantly changing operational environment to meet the emerging needs of the supported JFC. The joint logistics imperatives support the measurement of sustained logistics. These imperatives also build trust in the logistics process and between organizations during joint operations. These imperatives guide joint logisticians in the performance of the integrating functions needed for successful joint logistics operations.

a. **Unity of Effort.** Unity of effort is the coordination and cooperation toward common objectives, even if the participants are not necessarily part of the same command or organization; unity of effort is the product of successful unified action. For joint logisticians, unified action synchronizes and integrates logistic capabilities focused on the commander's intent. Unified action is critical to joint logistics outcomes. To achieve unity of effort, joint logisticians must develop a clear understanding of how joint and multinational logistics processes work, know the roles and responsibilities of the providers executing tasks in those processes, build agreement around common measures of performance, and ensure appropriate members of the JLEnt have visibility into the processes.

b. **JLEnt Visibility.** JLEnt visibility is access to logistic processes, resources, and requirements data to provide the information necessary to make effective decisions. JLEnt visibility is inclusive of the sub-components: AV, ITV, and the Defense Transportation System. AV is the ability to determine the location, movement, status, and identity of units, personnel, equipment, and supplies. It facilitates the capability to act upon information to improve overall performance of DOD logistics processes. ITV is the ability to track the identity, status and location of DOD units, and non-unit cargo (excluding bulk petroleum, oils, and lubricants [POL]) and passengers; patients; and personal property from origin to consignee or destination across the range of military operations. JLEnt visibility provides the means to share information and optimizes logistic capabilities to maximize outcomes, increase readiness, provide access to authoritative logistic information, and enable the user to respond quickly to the joint force's changing needs. Sharing data is essential to JLEnt visibility. Complete and timely information provides leaders and planners the ability to match available resources to operational demands. Visibility answers the commander's questions: What is it? Where is it? How and when will it arrive? To improve visibility and globally integrate operations, the JLEnt:

(1) Develops and enables common processes, methods, and language for JLEnt providers.

(2) Promotes policies that encourage transparency and the logistics community data owners to make their data accessible, interoperable, and secure.

(3) Cultivates global sourcing of resources among mission partners, across geographic boundaries, and among organizational affiliations to meet mission requirements.

(4) Pursues technology investments offering cost effective methods to advance logistics visibility in order to improve operational effectiveness.

c. **Rapid and Precise Response.** Rapid and precise response is the ability of the core logistic functions, military and commercial, to meet the constantly changing needs of the joint force. The effectiveness of joint logistics can be measured by assessing the following attributes, or key performance indicators.

(1) Speed is at the core of responsiveness. Speed does not mean everything moves at the same rate or fastest rate, but everything moves according to priority at the rate that produces the most effective support to the joint force.

(2) Reliability is reflected in the dependability of the global providers and the development of a resilient distribution network able to deliver required support when promised. Reliability is characterized by a high degree of predictability, or time-definite delivery of support. Time-definite delivery is the consistent delivery of requested logistics support at a time and destination specified by the requiring activity.

(3) Efficiency is related directly to the amount of resources required to achieve a specific outcome. In the tactical and operational environments, inefficiency increases the logistics footprint, force protection requirements, and risk. At the strategic level, inefficiency increases the cost and risk for the operation.

6. Logistics Integration

Commanders and staffs apply basic principles, control resources, and manage capabilities to provide sustained joint logistics. Logisticians can use the principles of logistics as a guideline to assess how effective logistics are integrated into plans and execution. To achieve full integration, commanders and their logisticians coordinate, synchronize, plan, execute, and assess logistic support to joint forces during all phases of the operation.

a. Principles of Logistics

(1) **Responsiveness.** Responsiveness is providing the right support when and where it is needed. Responsiveness is characterized by the reliability of support and the speed of response to the needs of the joint force. Clearly understood processes and well-developed decision support tools are key elements enabling responsiveness to emerging requirements. By monitoring the battle rhythm, the joint logistician can anticipate logistic issues and adjust to support operational needs.

(2) **Simplicity.** Simplicity fosters efficiency in planning and execution, and allows for more effective control over logistic operations. Clarity of tasks, standardized and interoperable procedures, and clearly defined command relationships contribute to simplicity. Simplicity is a way to reduce the "fog of war" or the friction caused by combat. Clear objectives, relevant processes, and documented procedures assist unity of effort.

(3) **Flexibility.** Flexibility is the ability to improvise and adapt logistic structures and procedures to changing situations, missions, and operational requirements. Flexibility is how well logistics responds in a dynamic environment. Where responsiveness is a commander's view of logistic support, flexibility is a logistician's view of being responsive. The logistician's ability to anticipate requirements in an operational environment allows for the development of viable options able to support operational needs.

(4) **Economy.** Economy is the minimum amount of resources required to bring about or create a specific outcome. Economy is achieved when support is provided using the

fewest resources within acceptable levels of risk. At the tactical and operational levels, economy is reflected in the number of personnel, units and equipment required to deliver support. Among the key elements of the logistic principle of economy is the identification and elimination of redundancy.

(5) **Attainability.** Attainability is the assurance that the essential supplies and services available to execute operations will achieve mission success. Attainability is the point at which the CCDR or subordinate JFC judges that sufficient supplies, support, distribution capabilities, and LOC capacity exist to initiate operations at an acceptable level of risk. Some examples of minimal requirements are inventory on hand (days of supply), critical support and Service capabilities, theater distribution assets (surge capability), combat service support (CSS) sufficiency, and force reception throughput capabilities.

(6) **Sustainability.** Sustainability is the ability to maintain the necessary level and duration of logistics support to achieve military objectives. Sustainability is a function of providing for and maintaining those levels of ready forces, materiel, and consumables necessary to support military action. Sustainability is focused on the long-term objectives and requirements of the supported forces. Sustainability provides the JFC with the means to enable freedom of action and extend operational reach.

(7) **Survivability.** Survivability is the capacity of an organization to prevail in spite of adverse impacts or potential threats. To provide continuity of support, critical logistic infrastructure must be identified and plans developed for its protection. Survivability is directly affected by dispersion, design of operational logistic processes, and the allocation of forces to protect critical logistic infrastructure. Examples of critical logistic infrastructure include industrial centers, airfields, seaports, railheads, supply points, depots, LOCs, bridges, intersections, logistic centers, and military installations.

b. **Coordinating and Synchronizing.** Effective coordination of joint logistics includes choosing organizational options to execute effective joint logistics operations.

Chapter III, "Coordinating and Synchronizing Joint Logistics," provides additional details on joint logistics control options.

c. **Planning.** Logistic planners at every level should set conditions for subordinate success. Timely, accurate, and responsive planning enables trade-offs, alternate courses of action (COAs), and therefore, freedom of action for JFCs. Joint logistics planning links the mission and commander's intent to core logistic functions, procedures, and organizations. This establishes the JFC's ability to meet requirements in terms of forces, capabilities, movement, projection, sustainment, duration of operations, redeployment, and retrograde.

Chapter IV, "Joint Logistics Planning," provides additional details.

d. **Executing.** Executing joint logistics involves the employment of capabilities and resources to support joint and multinational operations.

Chapter V, "Executing Joint Logistics," provides additional details.

e. **Assessing.**   Assessing joint logistics facilitates future success through plan refinement and adaptation. The joint logistician must be able to assess and respond to requirements by monitoring dynamic situations and providing accurate feedback to subordinates and decision makers.

7. Core Logistic Functions

Core logistic functions provide a framework to facilitate integrated decision making, enable effective synchronization and allocation of resources, and optimize joint logistic processes. The challenges associated with support cut across all core logistic functions, especially when multiple JTFs or multinational partners are involved. The core logistic functions are covered in detail in Chapter II, "Core Logistics Functions."

Intentionally Blank

CHAPTER II
CORE LOGISTICS FUNCTIONS

> *"Gentlemen, the officer who doesn't know his communications and supply as well as his tactics is totally useless."*
>
> **General George S. Patton, USA (1885-1945)**

1. Introduction

The previous chapter provided a joint logistics framework, and this chapter describes the core logistic functions. Each function includes people, processes, and resources. The core logistic functions are: deployment and distribution, supply, maintenance, logistic services, OCS, engineering, and HS. The core logistic functions are considered during the employment of US military forces in coordinated action toward a common objective and provide global force projection and sustainment (see Figure II-1).

2. Deployment and Distribution

The global dispersion of the threats, coupled with the necessity to rapidly deploy, execute, and sustain operations worldwide, makes the deployment and distribution capability the cornerstone of joint logistics. These operational factors necessitate a shift from a supply-based system to a system that is primarily distribution-based with beginning-to-end synchronization to meet JFC requirements. Through sharing critical information, it is possible to create unity of effort among diverse distribution organizations to satisfy deployment, execution, and sustainment operations. Reducing the joint logistics footprint provides JFCs with additional options to control the time and place of engagements, increased freedom to operate, and enhanced range, endurance, and agility of employed forces.

See JP 3-35, Deployment and Redeployment Operations, *and JP 4-09,* Distribution Operations, *for additional information.*

a. **Move the Force.** The Joint Staff J-3 is the DOD focal point to improve the joint deployment process. USTRANSCOM supports the deployment process during planning and execution by providing the strategic distribution capability to move forces and materiel in support of JFC operational requirements and to redeploy personnel, equipment, and materiel. As the DPO, USTRANSCOM coordinates and synchronizes this capability to transport units, equipment, and initial sustainment from the point of origin to the point of need and provides joint deployment and distribution enterprise (JDDE) resources to augment or support operational movement requirements of the JFC.

b. **Sustain the Force.** Sustaining the force consists of delivering non-unit related cargo and personnel. USTRANSCOM is responsible for coordinating and overseeing the DOD distribution system and collaborates with other logistics providers to move materiel through the distribution pipeline, from sourcing to the end user. Additionally,

Core Logistics Functions

Core Functions	Functional Capabilities
Deployment and Distribution	• Move the force • Sustain the force
Supply	• Manage supplies and equipment • Inventory management • Manage global supplier networks • Assess global requirements, resources, capabilities, and risks
Maintenance	• Depot maintenance operations • Field maintenance operations
Logistics Services	• Food service • Water and ice service • Contingency base services • Base and installations support • Hygiene services
Operational Contract Support	• Contract support integration • Contractor management
Engineering	• General engineering • Combat engineering • Geospatial engineering
Health Services	• Health service delivery • Force health protection • Health system support

Figure II-1. Core Logistics Functions

USTRANSCOM supports retrograde actions by moving non-unit equipment and materiel from the forward locations to a reset program or another directed operational area.

c. **Operate the JDDE.** The JDDE includes equipment, procedures, doctrine, leaders, technical connectivity, information, organizations, facilities, training, and materiel necessary to conduct joint deployment and distribution operations. The JDDE is a critical part of the JLEnt and its governance is the primary responsibility of the DPO in coordination with the Joint Staff J-3 and other members of the JDDE. USTRANSCOM, as DPO, exercises control of the JDDE through coordination and synchronization with

A helicopter, embarked aboard the aircraftcarrier USS Ronald Reagan (CVN 76), delivered humanitarian supplies throughout northern Japan in support of Operation TOMODACHI.

the community of interest (COI). Specifically, USTRANSCOM controls the JDDE, conducts JDDE operations, and protects the JDDE.

3. Supply

The joint logistician must understand the complexities of supply operations, the functions and processes that define them, and the organizations and personnel responsible for executing tasks in order to meet the JFC's requirements. DLA is primarily responsible for DOD supply chain operations and manages the supply process to provide common commodities and services to joint forces. Planning for supply operations requires a collaborative environment to fully consider all major components of the JLEnt to include the return and retrograde of equipment and supplies.

a. **Supply Chain.** The DOD supply chain is a global network that provides materiel, services, and equipment to the joint force. The fundamental goal of the supply chain is to understand the requirements, maximize force readiness and optimize the allocation of joint resources. The functional capabilities that contribute to the DOD supply chain include management of supplies and equipment, inventory management, management of global supplier networks, and assessment of global requirements, resources, capabilities, and risks. The DOD's supply chain responsiveness and reliability affects the readiness and capabilities of US military forces and is critical to the overall success of joint operations.

b. **Supply Chain Management.** Supply chain management involves identification and coordination of requirements, planning and synchronizing joint supply activities throughout DOD, and managing key global suppliers to support CCDR requirements. Critical elements of supply chain management include understanding and prioritizing requirements; visibility of forces as they maneuver, identifying mission-essential weapon systems and equipment; visibility of materiel moving through the distribution pipeline; ability to accurately forecast demands for sustainment; and prioritization of supply tasks in the area of responsibility (AOR). Operational planners can work with logistics planners to optimize supply chain operations and identify requirements to providers. Planners identify mission priorities, assess risks, and plan for the protection of the supply chain in the operational theater. Additional responsibilities include planning for disposition of hazardous materials, planning to retrograde material and equipment, and establishing JLEnt visibility of materiel requirements.

c. **Supply Chain Areas.** Joint logisticians must integrate all three areas of the DOD supply chain: managing supplies and equipment, managing inventory, and managing global supplier networks to provide responsive supply operations.

(1) **Manage Supplies and Equipment.** Joint logisticians integrate supply operations and work to increase supplier network performance to meet joint force demands. Logisticians should develop a seamless interface between supply operations from acquisition to delivery. Figure II-2 lists the classes and subclasses of supply managed by joint logisticians and their CUL suitability.

(2) **Inventory Management.** Inventory management is the process of managing, cataloging, determining requirements, procuring, distributing, overhauling, and disposing of materiel. Logisticians influence and employ inventory management to allow for the optimal balance of materiel in the supply chain to meet the issue and reclamation requirements of the end user. Managing inventory throughout the supply chain requires collaboration with supply and maintenance activities and distribution providers to enable the greatest effect at best value. Materiel inventory management capitalizes on accurate, real-time, and widely visible information and performance trends to inform decisions about attributes of the materiel inventory throughout the supply chain.

See Department of Defense Instruction (DODI) 3110.06, War Reserve Materiel (WRM) Policy, *for additional information.*

Classes, Subclasses of Supply, and Common-User Logistics Suitability

Class	Symbols	Subclass	Common-User Logistics (CUL) Capability
I. **Subsistence:** Food		A - Nonperishable dehydrated subsistence that requires organized dining facilities C - Combat rations includes meals, ready to eat (MREs) that require no organized dining facility; used in combat and in-flight environments. Includes gratuitous health and welfare items R - Refrigerated subsistence S - Non-refrigerated subsistence (less other subclasses) W - Water	Fully suited to CUL
II. **General Support Items:** Clothing, individual equipment, tentage, organizational tool sets and tool kits, hand tools, material, administrative, and housekeeping supplies		A - Air B - Ground support material E - General supplies F - Clothing and textiles G - Electronics M - Weapons T - Industrial supplies (e.g., bearings, block and tackle, cable, chain, wire, rope, screws, bolts, studs, steel rods, plates, and bars)	Limited CUL suitability
III. **Petroleum, Oils, Lubricants (POL):** Petroleum (including packaged items), fuels, lubricants, hydraulic and insulating oils, preservatives, liquids and compressed gasses, coolants, deicing, and antifreeze compounds, plus components and additives of such products, including coal		A - Air W- Ground (surface) P - Packaged POL	Excellent CUL candidate (with some limitations)
IV. **Construction/Barrier:** Materials that support fortification, obstacle and barrier construction, and construction material for base development and general engineering		A - Construction B - Barrier materials	Fully suited for CUL
V. **Ammunition:** Ammunition of all types (including chemical, radiological, and special weapons), bombs, explosives, mines, fuses, detonators, pyrotechnics, missiles, rockets, propellants, and other associated items		A - Air W - Ground	Limited, primarily to small arms, selected larger munitions

Figure II-2. Classes, Subclasses of Supply, and Common-User Logistics Suitability

Classes, Subclasses of Supply, and Common-User Logistics Suitability (Cont'd)

Class	Symbols	Subclass	Common-User Logistics (CUL) Capability
VI. Personal Demand Items: Nonmilitary sales items		A - Personal demand items not packaged as ration supplement sundry packs (RSSP) M- Personal and official letter and packaged mail. Does not include items in other classes such as spare parts P - RSSP	Fully suited for CUL
VII. Major End-Items: A final combination of end-products ready for intended use; e.g., launchers, tanks, racks, adapters, pylons, mobile machine shops, and administrative and tracked vehicles		A - Air B - Ground support material (includes power generators, fire-fighting, and mapping equipment) D - Administrative and general purpose vehicles (commercial vehicles used in administrative motor pools) G - Electronics J - Tanks, racks, adapters, and pylons (US Air Force only) K - Tactical and special purpose vehicles (includes trucks, truck-tractors, trailers, semi-trailers, etc.) L - Missiles M - Weapons N - Special weapons X - Aircraft engines	Not suitable for CUL
VIII. Medical Material/ Medical Repair		A - Medical material (including repair parts special to medical items) B - Blood and fluids	Fully suited for CUL
IX. Repair Parts (less medical special repair parts): All repair parts and components, including kits, assemblies, material power generators sub-assemblies (repairable and nonrepairable) required for all equipment; dry batteries		A - Air B - Ground support material, power generators, and bridging, fire-fighting, and mapping equipment D - Administrative vehicles (vehicles used in radio administrative motor pools) G - Electronics K - Tactical vehicles (including trucks, truck-tractors, trailers, semi-trailers, etc.) L - Missiles M - Weapons N - Special weapons T - Industrial supplies (e.g., bearings, block and tackle, cable, chain, wire, rope, screws, bolts, studs, steel rods, plates, and bars) X - Aircraft engines	Not suitable for CUL except for common items; requires special coordination to ensure proper support
X. (code as zero '0'): Material to support military programs, not included in classes I through IX	**CA**	None	Fully suited for CUL

Figure II-2. Classes, Subclasses of Supply, and Common-User Logistics Suitability (Cont'd)

(3) **Manage Global Supplier Networks.** A supply chain network is an engineered flow of information, funding or materiel from its suppliers to customers. Deployment and distribution capabilities are lynchpins in end-to-end supply chain management. Organizations provide data on the status of supplies and suppliers so logisticians can manage the JLEnt and adjust as necessary to the dynamics of operations.

See JP 3-35, Deployment and Redeployment Operations, *JP 4-01,* The Defense Transportation System, *and JP 4-09,* Distribution Operations, *for additional information.*

4. Maintenance

Maintenance supports system readiness for the JFC. The Services, as part of their Title 10, USC, responsibilities, execute maintenance as a core logistics function. The Services employ a maintenance strategy of depot and field level maintenance to improve the JFC's freedom of action and sustain the readiness and capabilities of assigned units. These levels of maintenance use various functional capabilities and processes to achieve their goal. Maintenance planning provides optimal availability of ready, reliable systems at best value.

a. **Depot Maintenance.** Depot level maintenance performs materiel maintenance requiring major overhaul, or a complete rebuilding of parts, assemblies, subassemblies, and end-items. Depot maintenance includes the manufacture of parts, modifications, testing, and reclamation as required, and provides a source of serviceable equipment and supports field maintenance by providing technical assistance or performing maintenance tasks beyond their responsibility. Depot maintenance is the most complex and extensive level of maintenance work and is a significant tie between the Nation's industrial base and military operations.

b. **Field Maintenance.** The purpose of field level maintenance is to return systems rapidly to users in a ready status. Field maintenance encompasses the organizational and on-system maintenance and repairs necessary for day-to-day operations as well as the intermediate, off-system repair of components and end items for weapons systems and supply chains. Field maintenance is less complex than depot level maintenance, and serves as the link between strategic capabilities and tactical requirements.

c. **Maintenance Personnel.** Depot and field maintenance personnel must possess the technical skills, tools, equipment, facilities, and an established quality assurance program to maintain equipment readiness. The following maintenance functions are performed at both depot and field locations:

(1) **Inspect.** Determines faults and verifies repairs or determines conditions by comparing characteristics to serviceability standards.

(2) **Test.** Evaluates the operational condition of end items and subsystems against established performance parameters.

(3) **Service.** Includes preventive maintenance checks and services, monitoring equipment health and conditions, and predictive maintenance to anticipate failures and diagnose faults.

(4) **Repair.** Restores items to serviceable status.

(5) **Rebuild.** Returns items to standards as close as possible to original conditions in appearance, performance, and life expectancy. This is the highest degree of materiel maintenance applied to equipment.

(6) **Calibrate.** Compares, adjusts, and validates systems of unknown accuracy to standards of known accuracy. If necessary and possible, adjustments are made to bring systems back into compliance with established performance standards.

d. **Maintenance Responsibility.** GCCs are responsible for the coordination of Service maintenance operations within their AORs. Functional CCDRs are responsible for the coordination of Service maintenance operations within their functional areas. CCDR requirements must be clear, and Service maintenance capabilities must be synchronized to provide the most effective materiel available to the joint force. Where practical, facilities for joint or cross-Service maintenance should be established, and inter-Service use of capabilities should be emphasized over single Service support. Lead Service or agency support, or in some cases multinational support options may also achieve more effective maintenance capabilities to support joint operations. These support options achieve greater synergy with systems common to two or more Services or multinational partners. Maintenance of ground systems, support equipment, communications electronics. and commercial systems can benefit from maintenance consolidation arrangements and can generate higher operational readiness, while reducing logistics footprint and cost.

e. **Equipment Reset.** Equipment deployed to a theater of operations must be periodically refurbished to meet current theater requirements. Equipment reset is a critical activity that restores a unit to a desired level of combat capability commensurate with its future mission. Equipment reset encompasses maintenance and supply activities that restore, reconstitute, and enhance the combat capability of unit and prepositioned equipment that has been destroyed, damaged, stressed, or worn out beyond economic repair due to operations. Equipment reset repairs or rebuilds the equipment to specified standards. When appropriate, it enhances existing equipment by inserting new technologies, restoring selected equipment to meet current or future operational demands, and/or procuring replacement equipment. Equipment reset is accomplished by both depot-level and field-level maintenance activities that perform major repairs, overhauls, and recapitalization (rebuilds or upgrade). Equipment reset is normally initiated with the rotation/return of equipment from an AOR. It may also be performed in theater when practical. Equipment reset of systems common to two or more Services may be performed under inter-Service arrangements when advantageous in terms of cost, logistics footprint, or operational readiness.

f. **Contractor Logistic Support (CLS).** CLS is another source of logistical support capabilities and is integral to providing service and material solutions to the warfighter for sustained operations. CLS is a method of obtaining logistics support for a product or service for a specified period of time. CLS could also include maintenance services and materiel provided under equipment warranty programs. In order to be effective, CLS must be planned and coordinated so that usage requirements are tracked, accountability is maintained, and tactical distribution requirements are met.

5. Logistic Services

Logistic services comprise the support capabilities that collectively enable the US to rapidly provide global sustainment for our military forces. Logistic services include many highly scalable and disparate capabilities. Included in this area are food service, water and ice service, contingency base services, hygiene services, and mortuary affairs (MA).

a. **Food Service.** Includes all aspects of dining facility management, subsistence procurement and storage, food preparation, food sanitation, and delivery to supported personnel.

b. **Water and Ice Service.** Includes capability to purify, test, store, and distribute bulk packaged and frozen water in a deployed environment. Water and ice for human consumption must meet potable water standards.

c. **Contingency Base Services.** Provides the assets, programs, and services necessary to support CCMD operations. This includes capabilities to operate, manage, and transition or close contingency locations for force application. Contingency locations provide shelter, billeting, utilities, common user life support management, force protection, and facility management (i.e., mayoral capability) in a deployed environment. The base operating support (BOS) functions of the personnel, equipment, services, activities, operational energy, and resources required to sustain operations at an installation are managed by a base operating support-integrator (BOS-I). A GCC may designate a Service component or JTF as the BOS-I at each contingency location. The BOS-I matrix in Appendix F, "Contingency Basing," is an example of how the CCDR can manage the various functions of BOS between Service components or PNs within a theater of operations from one base to another and within a single contingency base.

(1) **Real Property Life Cycle Management.** Provides acquisition, support, sustainment, recapitalization, disposal, and economic adjust activities for contingency base assets.

(2) **Support Services.** Deliver selected services to meet the requirements of the contingency location's population and mission. Support services provide security and emergency services, safety, base support vehicles and equipment, billeting services, airfield management, port services, range management, and space support services. These do not include services related to real property or personnel services.

d. **Hygiene Services.** Include both personal hygiene and textile services. Personal services provide adequate sinks, showers, and toilets to meet needs of both men and women. Textile services provide cleaning, repair, and return of clothing items and individual equipment.

e. **Mortuary Affairs (MA).** Provide care of deceased personnel for whom the Services are responsible by status and executive order beginning with the point of incident and ending at final disposition. MA include decontamination of contaminated remains.

For a more complete discussion of joint MA operations, see JP 4-06, Mortuary Affairs, *and Department of Defense Directive (DODD) 1300.22,* Mortuary Affairs Policy.

6. **Operational Contract Support**

DOD relies on contractors to perform many tasks. OCS provides the CCDR the tools and processes to manage the variety of services that may be required, such as base operational support, transportation, and security. Within OCS are contract support integration and contractor management.

a. **Contract Support Integration.** Contract support integration is the coordination and synchronization of contracted support executed in a designated operational area in support of the joint force. Effective contract support integration by the JFC maintains visibility of contracted capabilities.

b. **Contractor Management.** Contractor management is an expansive and complex process. It is the oversight and integration of contractor personnel and associated equipment providing support to the joint force in a designated operational area.

For further guidance on OCS, refer to JP 4-10, Operational Contract Support.

7. Engineering

Joint force engineers provide comprehensive recommendations to the commander on all engineering capabilities. They provide the ability to execute and integrate combat, general, and geospatial engineering to meet national and JFC requirements to assure mobility, provide infrastructure to position, project, protect, and sustain the joint force. Additionally, they enhance visualization of the operational area. The joint force engineer employs a combination of military engineers, civilians, contractors, and multinational and host nation (HN) capabilities to meet operational requirements, as well as BPC.

a. **General Engineering.** General engineering consists of engineer capabilities and activities, other than combat engineering, that modify, maintain, or protect the physical environment. Examples include the construction, repair, and maintenance of infrastructure, Class III/V storage area requirements, LOCs, and bases; protection of natural and cultural resources; real property life cycle support; terrain modification and repair; and selected explosive hazard activities.

b. **Combat Engineering.** Combat engineering consists of those engineer capabilities and activities that support the maneuver of land combat forces and requires close support to those forces. Combat engineering consists of three types of capabilities and activities: mobility, countermobility, and survivability. Examples include combined arms breaching operations, gap crossing operations, and constructing and maintaining combat roads and trails; development of barriers, obstacles, and minefields; and construction of fighting and protective positions.

c. **Geospatial Engineering.** Geospatial engineering consists of those engineering capabilities and activities that portray and refine data pertaining to the geographic location and characteristics of natural and constructed features and boundaries in order to provide engineering services to commanders and staffs. Examples include terrain analysis, terrain visualization, digitized terrain products, nonstandard tailored map products, precision survey, geospatial data management, baseline survey data, identification of significant cultural sites and natural resources, facility support, and force beddown analysis. Synchronizing the geospatial data provides the JFC the foundation to build a common operational picture (COP) that enhances awareness and decision making.

United States Army Corps of Engineers construct a community center in Varvarin, Serbia; a Marine electrician removes wood used to form a concrete ceiling in Bangladesh; Navy Seabees place concrete pieces at the Musa Qal'eh project in Afghanistan; An Airman balances on a communications tower in Westhampton Beach, New York.

For more information on joint engineering, refer to JP 3-34, Joint Engineer Operations, *and JP 3-15,* Barriers, Obstacles, and Mine Warfare for Joint Operations; *and for geospatial engineering, refer to JP 3-34,* Joint Engineer Operations, *and JP 2-03,* Geospatial Intelligence in Joint Operations.

8. Health Services

The purpose of HS is to improve the health readiness of individual personnel as well as the overall force and provide HS in order to ensure mission accomplishment. The CCDR requires scalable HS capabilities that are interoperable with other health programs, capable of rapid deployment into the operational area, and integrated across the Military Health System (MHS). HS includes all services performed, provided, or arranged that promote, improve, conserve, or restore the mental and physical wellbeing of personnel. HS employs a mix of MHS and Service capabilities in order to keep the force healthy and ready, maximizing the commander's freedom of action. HS is organized into three functional areas and can be found in greater detail in JP 4-02, *Health Services.*

a. **Force Health Protection (FHP).** FHP consists of capabilities which promote, improve, or conserve the mental and physical wellbeing of Service members. These capabilities enable a healthy and fit force, prevent injury and illness, and protect the force from health hazards.

b. **Health Service Delivery (HSD)** (formerly health service support). HSD consists of capabilities which provide timely appropriate quality healthcare to injured and ill personnel in order to restore mental and physical wellbeing. HSD includes diagnosis, treatment, rehabilitation, and reintegration of injured and ill personnel as well as casualty management in the operational area.

c. **Health System Support.** Health system support sustains and continuously improves the MHS mission effectiveness through the focused development of people, technology, infrastructure, contracts, and joint organizational culture. Health system support consists of managing the total medical force, health quality and safety, health education and training, medical financial management, medical/health information management, creating and sustaining the healing environment, joint and interagency medical logistics, and medical research and development.

CHAPTER III
COORDINATING AND SYNCHRONIZING JOINT LOGISTICS

"As we select our forces and plan our operations ...we must understand how logistics can impact on our concepts of operation...Commanders must base all their concepts of operations on what they know they can do logistically."

General Alfred M. Gray, Jr.
29th Commandant of the Marine Corps (July 1987-June 1991)

1. Introduction

This chapter describes the authorities, organizations, and control mechanisms that enable the synchronization of logistics in support of the JFC. JP 3-0, *Joint Operations,* identifies C2 as a joint function. Command includes both the authority and responsibility for effectively using available resources and the art of motivating and directing people and organizations to accomplish missions. Control is inherent in command. However, the logistic assets will rarely fall under one command, which makes control, coordination, synchronization, and management of joint logistics more challenging. To control joint logistics, commanders direct forces and functions consistent with a commander's command authority. It involves organizing the joint staff, operational level logistic elements, CSAs, and their capabilities to assist in planning and executing joint logistics. Designating lead Service, assigning agency responsibilities, and developing procedures to execute the CCDR's directive authority for logistics (DAFL) will assist in planning, integrating, synchronizing, and executing joint logistics support operations. While logistics remains a Service responsibility, there are other logistics organizations, processes, and tasks that must be considered when developing a concept of support in order to optimize joint logistics outcomes.

2. Logistics Authorities

a. **DAFL.** CCDRs exercise authoritative direction over logistics, in accordance with Title 10, USC, Section 164. DAFL cannot be delegated or transferred. However, the CCDR may delegate the responsibility for the planning, execution, and/or management of common support capabilities to a subordinate JFC or Service component commander to accomplish the subordinate JFC's or Service component commander's mission. For some commodities or support services common to two or more Services, the Secretary of Defense (SecDef) or the Deputy Secretary of Defense may designate one provider as the EA (see Appendix D, "Logistic-Related Executive Agents"). Other control measures to assist in developing common user logistics are joint tasks or inter-Service support agreements. However, the CCDR must formally delineate this delegated authority by function and scope to the subordinate JFC or Service component commander. The exercise of DAFL by a CCDR includes the authority to issue directives to subordinate commanders, including peacetime measures necessary for the execution of military operations in support of the following: execution of approved OPLANs; effectiveness and economy of operation; and prevention or elimination of unnecessary duplication of facilities and overlapping of functions among the Service component commands.

(1) During crisis action, wartime conditions, or where critical situations make diversion of the normal logistics process necessary, DAFL, when exercised by CCDRs, enables them to use all facilities and supplies of all forces assigned to their commands as necessary for the accomplishment of their missions. Joint logistic doctrine and policy developed by the Chairman of the Joint Chiefs of Staff (CJCS) establishes wartime logistic support guidance to assist the CCDR in conducting successful joint operations.

(2) The President or SecDef may extend this authority to attached forces when transferring forces for a specific mission, and should specify this authority in the establishing directive or order.

(3) A CCDR's DAFL does not:

(a) Discontinue Service responsibility for logistic support.

(b) Discourage coordination by consultation and agreement.

(c) Disrupt effective procedures or efficient use of facilities or organizations.

(d) Include the ability to provide contracting authority or make binding contracts for the United States Government.

(4) During peacetime, the scope of DAFL exercised by the CCDR is consistent with the legislative limitations, DOD policy or regulations, budgetary considerations, local conditions, and other specific conditions prescribed by SecDef or CJCS.

b. **DAFL Execution.** In exercising DAFL, CCDRs have an inherent obligation to ensure accountability of resources. This obligation is an acknowledgement of the Military Departments' Title 10, USC, responsibilities and recognizes that the Military Departments, with rare exceptions, do not resource their forces to support other DOD forces. In that regard, CCDRs will coordinate with appropriate Service components before exercising DAFL or delegating authority for subordinate commanders to exercise common support capabilities to one of their components. In keeping with the Title 10, USC, roles of the Military Departments, CCDRs should maintain an accounting of resources taken from one Service component and provided to another. This accounting can be used to reimburse the losing Service component in kind over time within the AOR when possible, or can be used to pass back a requirement to DOD for resource actions to rebalance Military Department resource accounts.

For more information on DAFL, refer to JP 1, Doctrine for the Armed Forces of the United States.

c. **EA.** A DOD EA is the head of a DOD component to whom SecDef or the Deputy Secretary of Defense has assigned specific responsibilities, functions, and authorities to provide defined levels of support for operational missions, or administrative or other designated activities that involve two or more of the DOD components. The DOD EA may delegate to a subordinate designee within that official's component, the authority to act on that official's behalf for any or all of those DOD EA responsibilities, functions, and authorities assigned by SecDef or the Deputy Secretary of Defense. The nature and scope of the DOD EA responsibilities, functions, and authorities shall be prescribed at the time of assignment and remain in effect until SecDef or the Deputy Secretary of Defense revokes or supersedes them. Only SecDef or the Deputy Secretary of Defense may designate a DOD EA and assign associated responsibilities, functions, and authorities within DOD.

See DODD 5101.1, DOD Executive Agent, *and Appendix D, "Logistics-Related Executive Agents," for details.*

d. **Lead Service.** The CCDR may choose to assign specific common user logistics functions, to include both planning and execution to a lead Service. These assignments can be for single or multiple common logistics functions, and may also be based on phases or locations within the AOR. In circumstances where one Service is the predominant provider of forces or the owner of the preponderance of logistics capability, it may be prudent to designate that Service as the joint logistics lead. Rarely does one Service's logistics organization have all the capabilities required to support an operation, so the CCDR may augment the lead Service logistics organization with capabilities from another component's logistics organizations as appropriate.

e. **BOS-I.** When multiple Service components share a common base of operations, the JFC may choose to designate a single Service component or JTF as the BOS-I for the location. The BOS-I facilitates unity of effort by coordinating sustainment operations at the location. This includes but is not limited to master planning, collecting and prioritizing construction requirements, seeking funding support, and force protection. When the base has a joint use airfield, the JFC also designates a senior airfield authority (SAA) responsible for airfield operations. When BOS-I and SAA are designated to different Services, close coordination of base support activities and airfield operations is essential.

3. **Joint Logistics Roles and Responsibilities**

Clearly articulating responsibilities is the first step in fully synchronized and coordinated logistics support during joint operations.

a. SecDef is the principal advisor to the President on defense matters and serves as the leader and chief executive officer of DOD. The offices of SecDef most concerned with logistics matters are the Under Secretary of Defense for Policy (USD[P]), Under Secretary of Defense for Acquisition, Technology, and Logistics (USD[AT&L]), and Assistant Secretary of Defense for Logistics and Materiel Readiness (ASD[L&MR]).

(1) **USD(P).** USD(P) is SecDef's principal staff assistant (PSA) and advisor for all matters on the formulation of national security and defense policy and the integration and oversight of DOD policy and plans to achieve national security objectives.

For more information on the USD(P), see DODD 5111.1, Under Secretary of Defense for Policy (USD[P]).

(2) **USD[AT&L].** The USD(AT&L) is the PSA and advisor to SecDef and Deputy Secretary of Defense for all matters relating to the DOD Acquisition System; research and

development; modeling and simulation; systems engineering; advanced technology; developmental test and evaluation; production; systems integration; logistics; installation management; military construction; procurement; environment, safety, and occupational health management; utilities and energy management; document services; and nuclear, chemical, and biological defense programs. The USD(AT&L) exercises authority, direction, and control over the DLA through the ASD(L&MR).

For more information on the USD(AT&L), see DODD 5134.01, Under Secretary of Defense for Acquisition, Technology, and Logistics (USD[AT&L]).

(3) ASD(L&MR) is the principal advisor to the USD(AT&L), SecDef, and Deputy Secretary of Defense on logistics and materiel readiness in DOD and is the principal logistics official within senior management.

For more information on the ASD (L&MR), see DODD 5134.12, Assistant Secretary of Defense for Logistics and Materiel Readiness (ASD [L&MR]).

(4) The Assistant Secretary of Defense for Operational Energy Plans and Programs (ASD[OEPP]) is the principal advisor to the USD(AT&L), SecDef, and Deputy Secretary of Defense and the principal policy official within the senior management of the DOD-regarding operational energy plans and programs.

For more information on the ASD(OEPP), see DODD 5134.15, Assistant Secretary of Defense for Operational Energy Plans and Programs (ASD[OEPP]).

b. The CJCS is the principal military adviser to the President and the National Security Staff (which consists of the National Security Council and the Homeland Security Council) and SecDef. CJCS prepares joint logistics and mobility plans to support strategic and contingency plans and recommends the assignment of logistics and mobility responsibilities to the Armed Forces. CJCS also advises SecDef on critical deficiencies in force capabilities (including manpower, logistics, intelligence, and mobility support).

c. **Military Departments.** The Military Departments exercise authority to conduct all affairs of their departments. These authorities include recruiting, organizing, supplying, equipping, training, servicing, mobilizing, demobilizing, administering, and maintaining forces; constructing, outfitting, and repairing military equipment; constructing, maintaining, and repairing buildings, structures, and utilities; and acquiring, managing, and disposing of real property or natural resources.

d. **Services.** The Army, Marine Corps, Navy, Air Force, and Coast Guard (when transferred to the Department of the Navy in accordance with Sections 2, 3, and 145 of Title 14, USC) are responsible for the functions enumerated in DODD 5100.01, *Functions of the Department of Defense and Its Major Components.* The components provide logistics support for Service and all forces assigned to joint commands, including procurement, distribution, supply, equipment, and maintenance, unless otherwise directed by SecDef.

For more information on the Military Departments, Services, and major components, see DODD 5100.01, Functions of the Department of Defense and Its Major Components.

e. **CCMDs.** Unless otherwise directed by the President or SecDef, the CCDR exercises authority, direction, and control over the commands and forces assigned to that command through combatant command (command authority) (COCOM). CCDRs are responsible for the coordination and approval of the aspects of administration, support (including control of resources and equipment, internal organization, and training) and discipline necessary to carry out missions assigned to the command.

For more information on the CJCS, Military Departments, Services, and CCMDs, see DODD 5100.1, Functions of the Department of Defense and Its Major Components.

f. **CSAs.** CSAs designated under Section 193 of Title 10, USC, fulfill combat support (CS) or CSS functions for joint operating forces across the range of military operations, and in support of CCDRs executing military operations. CSAs perform support functions or provide supporting operational capabilities, consistent with their establishing directives and pertinent DOD planning guidance. The USD(AT&L) is the PSA for DLA, the Defense Contract Management Agency (DCMA), and the Defense Threat Reduction Agency.

For more information on CSAs, see DODD 3000.06, Combat Support Agencies.

4. Combatant Commander's Logistics Directorate

The logistics directorate of a joint staff (J-4) at the CCMD is responsible for logistics planning and execution in support of joint operations. They perform this function by integrating, coordinating, and synchronizing Service component and CSA logistics capabilities to support the joint force. The J-4 also advises the JFC on logistics support to optimize available resources. Although the organizational considerations outlined below could apply to a CCDR's J-4 staff, they will most frequently be applied to subordinate joint force J-4 organizations. The J-4 staff supports the operations directorate of a joint staff (J-3) in the planning and executing of requirements for the joint reception, staging, onward movement, and integration (JRSOI) process as well as contingency base planning and sustainment. The J-4 coordinates, synchronizes, plans, and executes core logistics functions in joint and multinational environments.

a. **Planning.** The J-4 is responsible to provide logistics expertise as part of the joint operation planning process (JOPP). The J-4 establishes a logistics planning cell in coordination with the plans directorate of a joint staff (J-5), to fulfill this responsibility in accordance with JP 5-0, *Joint Operation Planning.* Planning occurs at every level of war in a networked, collaborative environment, which requires dialogue among senior leaders, concurrent and parallel plan development, and collaboration across multiple planning levels.

b. **Execution.** The geographic CCMD J-4 is responsible for coordinating and synchronizing joint theater logistics. This includes communicating the logistics priorities of the GCC to the Services responsible for executing joint logistics operations. The J-4s organize their logistics staff functions to respond to anticipated or ongoing operations.

c. **Joint Logistics Operation Center (JLOC).** The J-4 establishes a JLOC to monitor and control the execution of logistics in support of on-going operations. The JLOC is an integral part of the CCDR's operations element and provides joint logistics expertise to the J-3 operations cell. The JLOC is tailored to the operation and staffed primarily by the J-4 staff.

See Appendix C, "Joint Logistics Staff Organizations," for additional information on the JLOC.

d. **Joint Deployment and Distribution Operations Center (JDDOC).** At time of need a supported GCC can create a JDDOC and incorporate its capabilities into the staff functions. The GCC can place the JDDOC at any location required or under the operational control (OPCON) of other command or staff organizations. The JDDOC can reach back to the national partners to address and solve deployment and distribution issues for the GCC. The JDDOC develops deployment and distribution plans, integrates multinational and/or interagency deployment and distribution, and coordinates and synchronizes supply, transportation, and related distribution activities. The JDDOC synchronizes the strategic to operational movement of forces and sustainment into theater by providing advance notice to the GCC's air and surface theater movement C2 elements. In concert with the GCC's overall priorities, and on behalf of the GCC, the JDDOC coordinates common user and theater distribution operations above the tactical level. A joint movement center (JMC) may be established at a subordinate unified or JTF level to coordinate the employment of all means of transportation (including that provided by allies or HNs) to support the CONOPS. This coordination is accomplished through establishment of theater and JTF transportation policies within the assigned operational area, consistent with relative urgency of need, port and terminal capabilities, transportation asset availability, and priorities set by a JFC. The JTF JMC will work closely with the JDDOC.

For more information, see JP 4-09, Distribution Operations.

e. **Joint Logistics Boards, Centers, Offices, and Cells.** The CCDR may also establish boards, centers, offices, and cells (e.g., subarea petroleum office [SAPO], joint facilities utilization board [JFUB], joint mortuary affairs office [JMAO]) to meet increased requirements and to coordinate the logistics effort. Synchronizing and integrating the many joint logistics functional capabilities, multinational and interagency capabilities, and OCS may require the J-4 to establish a location or center where the requirements, resources, and processes can come together in a way that provides information to affect quality decision making. This fusion of information is essential to effective logistics support and critical to enabling the J-4 to see the logistics battlefield with clarity. These staff organizations are comprised of functional experts representing the joint logistics functions and provide functional assessments, analysis, and expertise to the planning and execution elements of the J-4.

See Appendix C, "Joint Logistics Staff Organizations," for additional information.

f. **Size.** The J-4's size is tailored to meet its mission requirements, and it is built around a core set of responsibilities described above in order to plan and execute the logistics operations for the JFC on a daily basis at the existing operating tempo. The core element is tailored to perform its functions under normal day-to-day conditions and provides the continuity and theater expertise to transition to an increased operating tempo should a CCDR move into a contingency or crisis.

5. Logistics Execution Organizations

The fundamental role of joint logistics is to integrate and coordinate logistics capabilities from Service, agency, and other providers of logistics support, and to facilitate execution of the Services' Title 10, USC, responsibilities while supporting the ever-changing needs of the JFC. Logistics may also be called upon to support the National Guard in their Title 32, USC, mission to execute DOD responsibilities for the Department of State program in support of security cooperation. It may also include special assignment airlift missions in addition to channel airlift, surface, and sealift movements. Joint logisticians should understand how each of the Services conducts logistics at the operational level.

a. **Army.** The overarching theater-level headquarters is the theater army/Army Service component command (ASCC), which provides support to Army forces and other Services as directed. It is important for the ASCC and theater special operations command (TSOC) J-4 to enhance conventional force and special operations forces (SOF) synchronization of sustainment. The theater sustainment command (TSC) is the logistics C2 element assigned to the ASCC and is the single Army logistics headquarters within a theater of operations. The TSC is responsible for executing port opening, theater opening, theater surface distribution, and sustainment functions in support of Army forces and provides lead Service and EA support for designated common user logistics to other government departments and agencies, multinational forces, and NGOs as directed. The TSC is also responsible for establishing and synchronizing the intratheater segment of the surface distribution system in coordination with the JDDOC with the strategic-to-theater segment of the global distribution network. The TSC rapidly establishes C2 of operational level logistics in a specified area of operations by employing one or more expeditionary sustainment commands (ESCs), which provides a rapidly deployable, regionally focused, forward-based C2 capability until a TSC can assume that function. When the Army is the predominant land force operating within an operational area, the TSC or ESC, at the discretion of the JFC, has the capability to become a joint logistics headquarters providing logistics support to all joint forces within the operational area. This is contingent upon the other Services, DOD agencies, and CCMDs providing the appropriate augmentation of personnel and capabilities to support this joint mission.

b. **Marine Corps.** The Marine expeditionary force (MEF) is the principle warfighting organization in the Marine Corps. A Marine logistics group (MLG) supports a MEF and is the largest Marine logistics element. An MLG organizes and deploys rapidly to meet MEF mission requirements. While the Marine Corps is not normally tasked to execute operational level logistics, the Marine Corps component commander may be augmented and/or may task elements of a logistics combat element to perform operational-level functions. Integration with strategic level logistics support is coordinated through the Marine Corps component commander.

c. **Navy.** For numbered fleets, the senior logistician is both the assistant chief of staff for logistics and the logistics readiness center (LRC) director. Coordination and unity of effort between the LRC and logistics supporting staffs and commands providing logistics resources and support is key to effectively controlling and executing logistics support.

(1) The logistics forces of each numbered fleet are organized into standing task forces, and the commanders of these task forces are the principal logistic agents for the fleet commander. The logistics task force commander is responsible to the fleet commander for management of logistics support forces for maritime sustainment of Navy, Coast Guard, and Marine Corps units. The logistics task force commander has tactical control of Military Sealift Command Combat Logistics Force ships; plans resupply of resupply of all classes of supply; and plans and manage theater ship repairs in military and commercial yards outside the continental US.

(2) Fleet operational forces are normally organized into task forces under the command of a task force commander. The task force commander exercises control of logistics through a fleet logistics coordinator, task force logistics coordinator, or task group logistics coordinator who in turn normally exercises OPCON of assigned combat logistics forces and is responsible for coordinating the replenishment of forces at sea.

d. **Air Force.** The air and space expeditionary task force (AETF) is the organizational structure for deployed US Air Force forces. AETF presents a scalable, tailorable organization with three elements: a single commander, embodied in the commander, Air Force forces (COMAFFOR); appropriate C2 mechanisms; and tailored and fully supported forces. The Air Force forces staff is the vehicle through which the COMAFFOR fulfills operational and administrative responsibilities for assigned and attached forces, and is responsible for long-range planning that occurs outside the air tasking cycle. Director of manpower, personnel, and services (A-1); director of logistics (A-4); director of installations and mission support (A-7); and surgeon general (SG) are PSAs to the COMAFFOR for JOA-wide integration of agile CS capabilities and processes. A-1 is responsible for the functions of billeting, MA assistance, and food service to include bottled water to support planned meals. Responsibility for planning daily consumable water outside of planned meals resides with A-7, civil engineering. Contracting is the responsible agent to procure bottled water (when the requirements have been established) from approved sources that are coordinated with US Army Veterinary Command and/or bioenvironmental engineers and public health. A-4/7 controls logistics planning, distribution, aerial port, material management, fuels, maintenance, and munitions, civil engineering, fire emergency services, explosive ordnance disposal, chemical, biological, radiological, and nuclear defense and response elements of emergency management; contracting; and force protection. The SG advises on FHP and HSD. In general, these Air Force directorates formulate and implement policies and guidance to ensure effective support to Air Force forces. It is important to recognize that many joint logistics functions typically associated with the J-4 are divided between multiple Air Force directorates.

e. **Coast Guard.** Coast Guard deployable units are capable of providing combat and CS forces and are able to react rapidly to worldwide contingencies. In order to accomplish the many missions, deployable units and assets consist of high endurance cutters, patrol boats, buoy tenders, aircraft, port security units, maritime safety and security teams, maritime security response teams, tactical law enforcement teams, and the National Strike Force. Logistics support is provided through the Coast Guard Surface Forces Logistic Center and their subordinate elements. When Coast Guard units operate as part of a JTF, Coast Guard units may draw upon the logistics support infrastructure established by/for the JTF. These general support functions normally include but are not limited to the following: berthing, subsistence, ammunition, fuel, and accessibility to the naval supply systems. The Navy logistics task force commander is responsible for coordinating the replenishment, intratheater organic airlift, towing, and salvage, ship maintenance, and material control, as well as commodity management for the task force group.

f. **SOF.** Commander, United States Special Operations Command (CDRUSSOCOM) exercises COCOM over all SOF. As directed, GCCs exercise OPCON over assigned TSOC and their subordinate JFCs to include attached SOF.

(1) When a GCC establishes and employs multiple JTFs and independent task forces, the commander, theater special operations command (CDRTSOC) may establish and employ multiple joint special operations task forces (JSOTFs) and special operations command-forward to control SOF assets and accommodate JTF/task force special operations requirements. Accordingly, the GCC normally will establish supporting or tactical control command relationships between JSOTF commanders and JTF/task force commanders. When directed, CDRUSSOCOM can establish and employ a JSOTF as a supported commander. The CDRTSOC and JSOTF J-4s are the primary logistics control authorities for SOF. Responsibilities include oversight of the core logistic functions. The JSOTF J-4 must ensure that JSOTF forces are supported by the Services, which is required by Title 10, USC. The JSOTF J-4 is dependent on Service and joint logistics support as the primary means of support. The JSOTF J-4 may have to recommend and/or set priorities of support for common user items and consolidated functions. Limited resources available to the JSOTF elements may require the J-4 to provide prioritization information to the JTF J-4 and/or the appropriate lead Service logistics organization.

(2) In addition to the core logistic functions, special operations-peculiar support must be considered. This support includes equipment, materials, supplies, and services required for special operations missions for which there is no Service-common requirement. These are limited to items and services initially designed for, or used by, SOF until adopted for Service-common use by one or more Service; modifications approved by CDRUSSOCOM for application to standard items and services used by the Services; and items and services approved by the CDRUSSOCOM as critically urgent for the immediate accomplishment of a special operations mission. This support will be provided via United State Special Operations Command (USSOCOM) Service component logistics infrastructures and in coordination with theater Service components. Logistics support to SOF units is the responsibility of each Service's logistics C2 structure, and this responsibility exists regardless of whether the SOF unit requiring support is assigned to the Service component, the TSOC, JSOTF, military information support operations task force, or a joint civil-military operations task force. The GCC will ensure appropriate Service logistic support is made available to the JSOTF through one of the logistics control options described in paragraph 6, "Logistic Control Options," of Chapter III, "Coordinating and Synchronizing

Joint Logistics." For rapid response operations, USSOCOM component commands will maintain the capability to support SOF elements for an initial period of 15 days. Services and/or EAs should be prepared to support special operations as soon as possible but not later than 15 days after SOF are employed.

g. **USTRANSCOM.** Serves as the global distribution synchronizer, as outlined in the Unified Command Plan, on behalf of and in coordination with the JDDE COI to establish processes to plan, apportion, allocate, route, schedule, validate priorities, track movements, and redirect forces and supplies per the supported commander's intent. This coordination and synchronization will not infringe upon either the supported CCDRs, or Services Title 10, USC, designated responsibilities, but serves to facilitate a unity of effort throughout the JDDE to support the CCDR or subordinate JFC. The supported GCC is responsible to plan, identify requirements, set priorities, and redirect forces and sustainment as needed to support operations within the respective AOR. USTRANSCOM, as the Mobility Joint Force Provider, exercises responsibility for planning, resourcing, and operating a worldwide defense transportation system in support of distribution operations, to include reviewing taskings and analyzing supported CCDR's requirements for transportation feasibility, and advising on changes required to produce a sustainable force deployment. During the deployment, sustainment, and redeployment phases of a joint operation, CCDRs coordinate their movement requirements and required delivery dates with USTRANSCOM, and supported GCCs are responsible for deployment and distribution operations executed with assigned/attached force in their respective AORs.

(1) USTRANSCOM may also sponsor or provide other distribution process enablers, to include JDDOC, augmentation, and joint task force-port opening (JTF-PO). Although all Services have the organic capability to execute theater opening functions, among other logistics tasks such as port opening and distribution, the JTF-PO provides a joint expeditionary capability to rapidly establish and initially operate an aerial or sea port of debarkation (POD). From the POD, JTF-PO conducts cargo handling and port clearance/movement control to a forward distribution node, facilitating port throughput in support of GCC executed contingencies. JTF-PO will normally operate within a theater over a 45-60 day time frame before having to be replaced by forces arriving via the time-phased force and deployment data (TPFDD) process. It will be important early on for the GCC, subordinate commanders, and USTRANSCOM to establish a closely coordinated transition plan (relief in place or transfer of authority) to ensure the smooth continuity of both aerial and sea PODs operations.

(2) JTF-PO also supports USTRANSCOM's mission of providing end-to-end synchronized cargo and passenger movement and common-user terminal management. JTF-PO is designed to be in place in advance of a deployment of forces, sustainment, or humanitarian/relief supplies in order to facilitate joint reception, staging, onward movement, integration and theater distribution. This is accomplished by providing an effective interface between the theater JDDOC, associated POD, and other organizations. When JTF-PO is utilized, Commander, United States Transportation Command (CDRUSTRANSCOM), will retain OPCON over forces in most cases while in theater. USTRANSCOM will require support from the GCC in order to execute this capability (e.g., force protection, life support, communications, and real estate).

(3) As the force provider for joint enabling capabilities, CDRUSTRANSCOM, through the Joint Enabling Capabilities Command (JECC), provides mission-tailored, ready joint capability packages, as directed, which are capable of short-notice, limited duration deployments to assist CCDRs in establishing, organizing, and operating a joint forces headquarters, including deployable communications and public affairs support. When requested, JECC's Joint Planning Support Element (JPSE) provides a flexible employment package composed of personnel, including logisticians, who are experienced in the planning and execution of the full range of joint military operations. JPSE logisticians maintain expertise in the integration, coordination, and implementation of joint logistics operations and planning to support joint operations.

For additional information on the JECC, see JP 3-33, Joint Task Force Headquarters.

h. **DLA.** DLA manages, integrates, and synchronizes suppliers and supply chains to support the Armed Forces of the US, allies, and multinational partners. The ASD(L&MR), under the USD(AT&L), exercises authority, direction, and control over DLA. As a statutory CSA, DLA provides logistics advice and assistance to the Office of the Secretary of Defense, the CJCS, Joint Chiefs of Staff, the CCDRs, Military Departments, DOD components, and interagency partners, as appropriate. Additionally, DLA operates as part of the JLEnt in providing humanitarian assistance. DLA manages nine diverse supply chains and serves as the DOD EA for four supply chains: subsistence, construction and barrier materiel, bulk petroleum, and medical materiel. DLA also directs a network of distribution depots located throughout the US, Europe, Pacific, and South West Asia. These depots stock a wide range of commodities owned by the Services, General Services Administration, and DLA. Equally important are DLA's capabilities for conducting reutilization and disposition of end items, repair parts, hazardous property, and hazardous waste. DLA has a global presence and operates regional commands in US Central Command, US Pacific Command, US European Command, and US Africa Command, and has liaison officers attached to the remaining CCMD staffs and the Joint Staff to assist with operation planning, exercises, and current operations. In addition, DLA support teams provide logistics products and services to warfighters worldwide in support of military operations.

i. **DCMA.** DCMA is the CSA responsible for ensuring major DOD acquisition programs (systems, supplies, and services) are delivered on time, within projected cost or price, and meet performance requirements. DCMA's major role and responsibility in contingency operations is to provide contingency contract administration services for external and theater support contracts. DCMA is also responsible for selected weapons system support contracts with place of performance in the operational area and theater support contracts when contract administration services are delegated by the procuring contracting officers.

j. **Defense Security Cooperation Agency (DSCA).** DSCA arranges DOD funded and space available transportation for NGOs for delivery of humanitarian goods to countries in need; coordinates foreign disaster relief missions; and, in concert with DLA, procures, manages, and arranges for delivery of humanitarian daily rations and other humanitarian materiel in support of US policy objectives.

6. Logistics Control Options

The CCDR's logistics authority enables use of all logistics capabilities of the forces assigned as necessary for the accomplishment of the mission. The President or SecDef may extend this authority to attached forces when transferring those forces for a specific mission and should specify this authority in the establishing directive or order. The CCDR may elect to control logistics through the J-4 staff tailored and augmented as discussed in paragraph 4, "Combatant Commander's Logistics Directorate." The CCDR may also decide to control joint logistics by designating a subordinate logistics organization. In these instances, the CCDR will delineate the authorities and command relationships that will be used by the subordinate commander to control logistics. In both cases, the CCDR exercises effective control of joint force logistics by fusing procedures and processes to provide visibility and control over the logistics environment, and integrating joint logistics planning with operations planning. Control of joint logistics is enhanced by how effectively the logistician combines the capabilities of the global providers and the Service's logistics elements with the JFC's requirements in a way that achieves unity of effort.

a. **Staff Control.** The J-4 staff may be used to support a wide range of operations including campaigns; complex or long duration major operations; or complex operations involving multiagency, IGO, NGO, or multinational forces, if properly augmented. For example, the staff may be sized and tasked to provide increased movement control or material management capabilities; it could be augmented with a robust OCS planning and integration capability; the J-4 could receive augmented capability to coordinate multinational support operations or execute JOA-wide infrastructure repair/restoration missions. J-4 staff augmentation can come from a combination of military, civilian emergency workforce, and contractor personnel. When exercising this option the CCDR will specify the control authorities delegated to the J-4 over the components logistics elements. Taskings to Service component logistics elements in this case must come from formal tasking orders issued through the CCDR's J-3. The logistics taskings, which could come in the form of a fragmentary order (FRAGORD), formalizes the authorities given the J-4 by the JFC, and enables the rapid response to operational logistics requirements.

b. **Organizational Control.** As another alternative for controlling the major operations outlined above, the CCDR may elect to assign responsibility to establish a joint command for logistics to a subordinate Service component. The senior logistics headquarters of the designated Service component will normally serve as the basis for this command, an organization joint by mission (e.g., campaigns, major operations, humanitarian missions), but not by design. When exercising this option, the CCDR retains DAFL, and must specify the control and tasking authorities being bestowed upon the subordinate joint command for logistics, as well as the command relationships it will have with the Service components. This command would control logistics taskings as directed by the CCDR and must not infringe on the authorities and responsibilities as specified in paragraph 3, "Joint Logistics Roles and Responsibilities." The CCDR would augment this joint command as required with joint, agency, and other Service capabilities to effectively integrate and control logistics requirements, processes and systems, and with forces made available.

c. **CUL Control**

(1) Planners should consider areas where CUL organizational options are best suited. CCMD and subordinate logistic planners must keep in mind that while CUL support can be very efficient, it may not always be the most effective method of support. By its very nature, CUL support will normally take place outside routine support channels, which may lead to reduced responsiveness if not properly planned, coordinated, and executed. CCDRs, along with their subordinate commanders, must review, coordinate, and direct CUL requirements with DLA, functional CCDRs, and Service component commanders to provide an integrated joint logistic system from the strategic to tactical levels. All parties must ensure that the advantages and disadvantages of each CUL-related COA are properly considered; however, the GCC has overall responsibility for deciding the amount and type of CUL support for a particular joint operation. The CCDR's decision to use DAFL to direct CUL support within a subordinate joint force must be deliberate and coordinated to ensure proper CUL execution. Key elements that CCDRs and subordinate JFCs must consider when establishing CUL responsibility are:

(a) Done deliberately.

(b) Involves only common support items.

(c) Requires item visibility.

(d) Normally does not come from tactical unit stocks.

(e) Must have specific reimbursement procedures in place.

(2) **Cross-Leveling CUL Assets.** It must be clearly understood that only the CCDR has the authority to direct the cross-leveling of supplies within a joint force. Cross-leveling of a supply for one Service component will be only for common items and should be accomplished in a very prudent and deliberate manner. CUL suitability for commodities is displayed in Figure III-1, as well as other potential CUL areas that should be considered in reducing redundancy, risks, and costs.

(3) **Organizational Control Options.** Based on the operational situation, the CCDRs can modify or mix two major control options: single-Service logistic support or lead Service/agency support.

(a) **Single-Service Logistic Support.** In this organizational option, each Service retains primary responsibility for providing support to their subordinate organizations. CUL would be limited to existing support relationships between Services as identified in inter-Service support agreements. If delegated by the CCDR, the J-4 may coordinate limited CUL support to other Services or agencies in certain situations. This method would most likely be used in major operations where the operational situation allows for, and calls for, the deployment of the requisite Service component logistics assets in a timely manner and where logistic effectiveness is paramount.

(b) **Lead Service or Agency CUL Support.** The CCDR may designate a lead Service or DOD agency to provide selected CUL support to one or more Service components, governmental organizations, and/or NGOs in a joint or multinational operation.

This CUL option is normally based on the dominant user and/or most capable Service concepts and may or may not involve OPCON or tactical control of one Service component logistic units to the lead Service.

Potential Common-User Logistics Areas and Sustainability

Type of Service	Common-User Logistics Sustainability	Potential Common-User Logistics Areas
Maintenance and Salvage	Very Limited	Common Ground Equipment Communications Electronics Salvage
Transportation	Good	Port Opening Material Handling Equipment Common Airlift Support Common Sealift Support Common Port Operation Support Common Land Transportation Movement Control Logistics Over-The-Shore Joint Reception, Staging, Onward Movement, and Integration Noncombatant Evacuation Operations
Develop and Maintain Facilities	Excellent	Base Development Environmental Support
Hazardous Material and Waste Management	Excellent	Inventory Management Disposal
Health Services	Excellent	Medical Evacuation Hospitalization Blood Management Veterinary Services Dental Services Preventative Medicine Medical Logistics Medical Laboratory Services Vector Control Behavioral Health Services
Other Services	Excellent	Mortuary Affairs Reutilization and Disposal Explosive Ordnance Disposal Water Support Food Service Support Laundry and Shower Support Clothing and Textile Repair Contingency Base Support Other contracted support Post or base exchange support

Figure III-1. Potential Common-User Logistics Areas and Sustainability

d. **Control Option Selection Considerations.** After determining what commodities and functions will be joint, the CCDR must decide how to control those logistic operations. The selection of a control option should benefit from a careful analysis to include the following considerations. These considerations are not designed to stand alone. They should be considered comprehensively in order to properly inform the commander's decision.

(1) **Mission.** The mission is the foremost consideration from the commander when selecting the option that will be used to control joint logistics. Mission analysis helps identify the complexity and scale of the joint logistics requirements the command will face during execution. Generally, the more complex operations have greater need for an organizational control option.

(2) **The Most Capable Service Component.** This consideration aligns with the most prevalent Service capabilities in the operational area. It is one of the most important considerations to analyze because no Service component's logistics organization is staffed or equipped to plan and execute joint logistics. To some degree the most capable Service component organization will have to be augmented to provide common-user support responsibilities. Without adequate Service component logistics C2 capability available, the staff control option would be the most appropriate.

(3) **The Geographic and Physical Infrastructure in the Operational Area.** This consideration is related to the most capable Service component consideration. The geographic and physical infrastructure in the operational area usually dictates the nature of the LOCs needed to support the joint force and the need for intermediate support bases or platforms. The LOCs will influence the distribution system to include the location of distribution points and the challenges brought on by the ITV technology need to support the operation. Additionally, the condition of the LOCs may force common user logistics, common user land transport, and intratheater plans. The GCC should coordinate with USTRANSCOM, DOD agencies, and other stakeholders when analyzing the geography and physical infrastructure in the operational area, and when selecting the control option.

(4) **GCC Option Selection and Design.** Figure III-2 details a logical sequence that can be used by GCCs when evaluating, selecting, and designing the option they will use to control joint logistics. For more amplifying information detailing the joint logistics factors and enablers with regard to the staff and organization control options, see Appendix E, "Geographic Combatant Commander Logistics Control Factors and Tools Available."

7. **Technology**

The rapid advance of technology, if leveraged effectively, can enable the JFC to effectively control logistics within the operational area. Technology, in the form of information systems, decision support tools, and evolving communications capabilities can improve visibility of logistics processes, resources, and requirements and provide the information necessary to make effective decisions. These technologies can also contribute to a shared awareness that enables the JFC to focus capabilities against the joint forces most important requirements, and can be used to more effectively capture source data, make data more accessible within the public domain, and integrate data into tools or applications that enable effective decision making.

Logistics operations rely on a variety of Service and agency information systems to gather the data necessary for planning, decision making, and assessment.

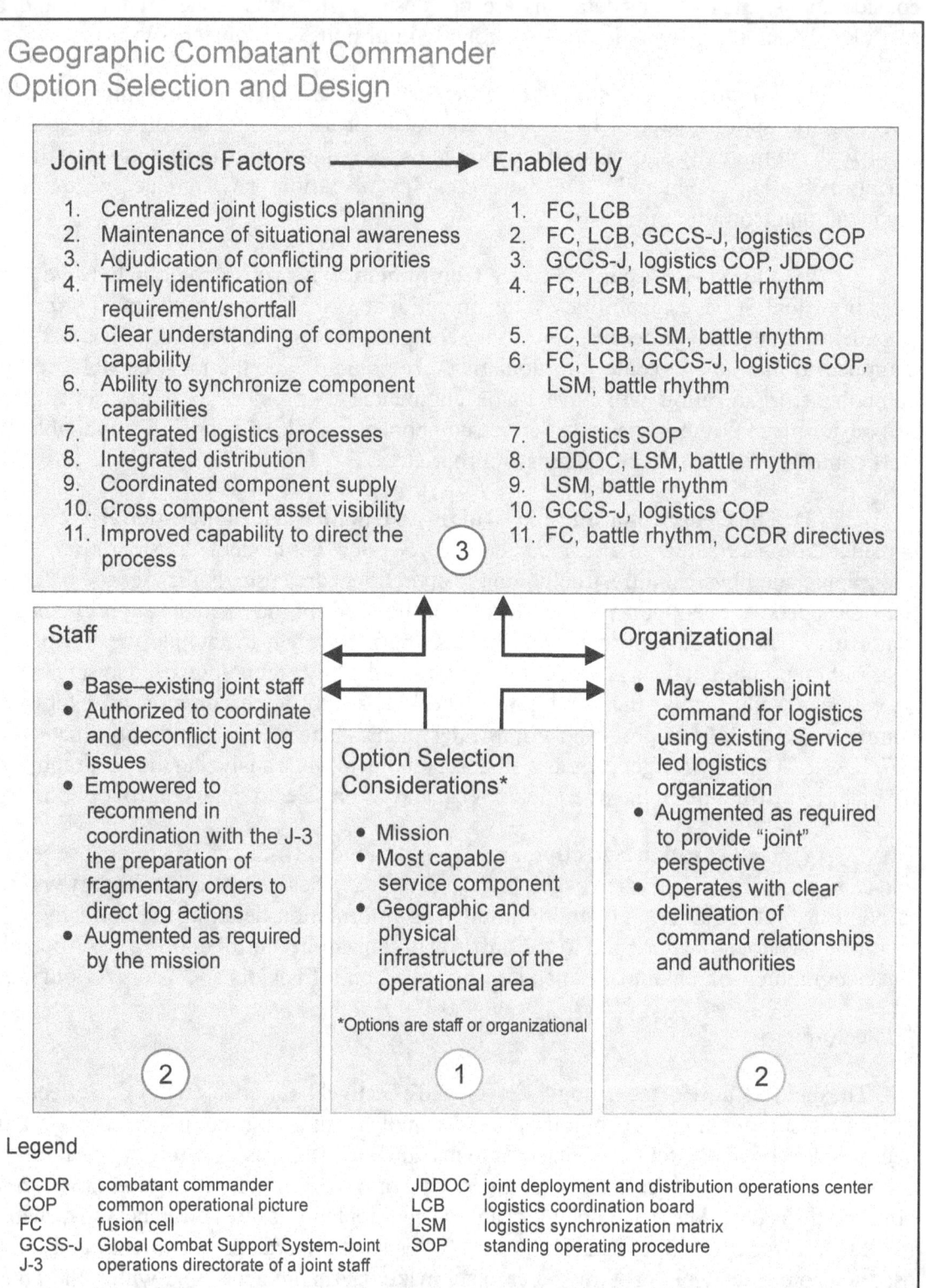

Figure III-2. Geographic Combatant Commander Option Selection and Design

a. **The Global Combat Support System-Joint (GCSS-J).** GCSS-J is an authoritative information technology application used to provide automation support to the joint logistician. In order to deliver visibility over resources, requirements, and capabilities, GCSS-J uses a service-orientated architecture to link the joint logistician to component, Service, multinational, and other agencies, allowing all concerned to use shared data to plan, execute, and control joint logistic operations. It provides the terminal operator visibility of mobilization, deployment, employment, sustainment, redeployment, and demobilization information through the use of a portal and Web-based applications that deliver enhanced visibility and is available on both the SECRET Internet Protocol Router Network (SIPRNET) and Nonsecure Internet Protocol Router Network (NIPRNET).

b. **Logistics Information Management and Sharing.** The DOD components contribute critical information that support the CCDRs' logistics planning and COP by providing ITV, and AV. The CCDRs' information needs are being supported by DOD components' use of technologies to facilitate effective and efficient JLEnt visibility. One example is a forecasting model, the Integrated Consumable Item Support model, a SIPRNET web-based planning application that forecasts OPLAN requirement demands Class I, III, and IX sustainment. This and other inputs per the Joint Reporting System assist the CCMDs and Service components in development of logistics supportability analysis (LSA) for those OPLANs with a TPFDD and annex D (Logistics) for component support plans.

8. Multinational and Interorganizational

Multinational and interorganizational operational arrangements regarding joint logistics are bound together by a web of relationships among global providers. These relationships are critical to joint logistics success because logistics capabilities, resources, and processes are vested in a myriad of organizations which interact across multiple physical domains and the information environment, and span the range of military operations.

a. **Multinational Operations.** In today's operational environment, logisticians will likely be working with multinational partners. While the US maintains the capability to act unilaterally, it is likely that the requirement, and the desire, to operate with multinational partners will continue to increase. Multinational logistics is a challenge; however, leveraging multinational logistics capabilities increases the CCDR's freedom of action. Additionally, many multinational challenges can be resolved or mitigated by having a thorough understanding of the capabilities and procedures of our multinational partners before operations begin. Integrating and synchronizing logistics in a multinational environment requires multinational information sharing, developing interoperable logistics concepts and doctrine, as well as clearly identifying and integrating the appropriate logistics processes, organizations, and C2 options. Careful consideration should be given to the broad range of multinational logistics support structures.

For further reference on multinational logistics, refer to JP 4-08, Logistics in Support of Multinational Operations.

b. **Interorganizational.** Integration and coordination among military forces, other government departments and agencies, NGOs, and IGOs is different from the coordination requirements of a purely military operation. These differences present significant challenges to coordination. First, the government department or agency/NGO/IGO culture is different from that of the military. Their operating procedures will undoubtedly differ from one organization to another and with DOD. However, their similar needs (e.g., distribution, materials handling equipment, shelter, water, and power) in a contingency environment will add another requirement for resources that must be addressed early in any operation. Ultimately, some government departments and agencies, NGOs, and IGOs may even have policies not in consonance with those of DOD. In the absence of a formal command structure, the joint logistician will need to collaborate and elicit cooperation to accomplish the mission. NGOs and IGOs possess unique skills and capabilities that can assist in providing the joint warfighter more robust logistics.

For additional information on logistics support during IGO and NGO coordination efforts, refer to JP 3-08, Interorganizational Coordination During Joint Operations. *For additional information on civil-military operations, refer to JP 3-57,* Civil-Military Operations.

A CH-46 helicopter flies past the amphibious dock landing ship USS Tortuga and the Royal Thai Navy medium landing ship HTMS Surin during Exercise COBRA GOLD 2012, a Thai-US co-sponsored joint and multinational exercise designed to advance security throughout the Asia-Pacific region and enhance interoperability with participating nations.

CHAPTER IV
JOINT LOGISTICS PLANNING

"Logistics considerations belong not only in the highest echelons of military planning during the process of preparation for war and for specific wartime operations, but may well become the controlling element with relation to timing and successful operation."

Vice Admiral Oscar C. Badger, United States Navy
Address to the Naval War College, 1954

1. Introduction

Joint logistics planning provides the process and the means to integrate, synchronize, and prioritize joint logistics capabilities toward achieving the supported commander's operational objectives and desired outcome during all phases of plan development. This chapter is applicable for global or theater campaign plans, subordinate campaign plans, campaign support plans, and deliberate plans tasked in the Chairman of the Joint Chiefs of Staff Instruction (CJCSI) 3110, *Joint Strategic Capabilities Plan (JSCP) series*, or as directed by the CCDR. This chapter also addresses planning considerations, input and output products used by joint logisticians to create OPLANs/operation orders (OPORDs) that enable transition from peacetime activities to execution of orders. Focus is on JOPP in development of the theater logistics overview (TLO) as a segment of the theater campaign plan (TCP).

a. The requirement to perform joint logistics planning is derived from Title 10, USC, Section 153, *Guidance for Employment of the Force (GEF)*, JSCP, and guidance provided in the JSCP directed supplements and/or coordinating instructions.

b. Joint logistics planning is conducted under the construct of joint operation planning and the associated JOPP addressed in JP 5-0, *Joint Operation Planning*. Joint operation planning consists of planning activities associated with joint military operations by CCDRs and their subordinate commanders in response to contingencies and crises. It transforms national strategic objectives into activities by development of operational products that include planning for the mobilization, deployment, employment, sustainment, redeployment, and demobilization of joint forces. Joint operation planning occurs at multiple strategic national and operation levels using process, procedures, tactics, techniques and facilitating information technology tools/applications/systems aligned to the Joint Operation Planning and Execution System (JOPES) and its transition to the Adaptive Planning and Execution (APEX) system.

2. Planning Functions

a. Joint operation planning encompasses a number of elements, including four planning functions: strategic guidance, concept development, plan development, and plan assessment (see Figure IV-1). Depending upon the type of planning and time available, these functions can be sequential or concurrent. Joint operation planning features detailed planning guidance and frequent dialogue between senior leaders and commanders to promote a common

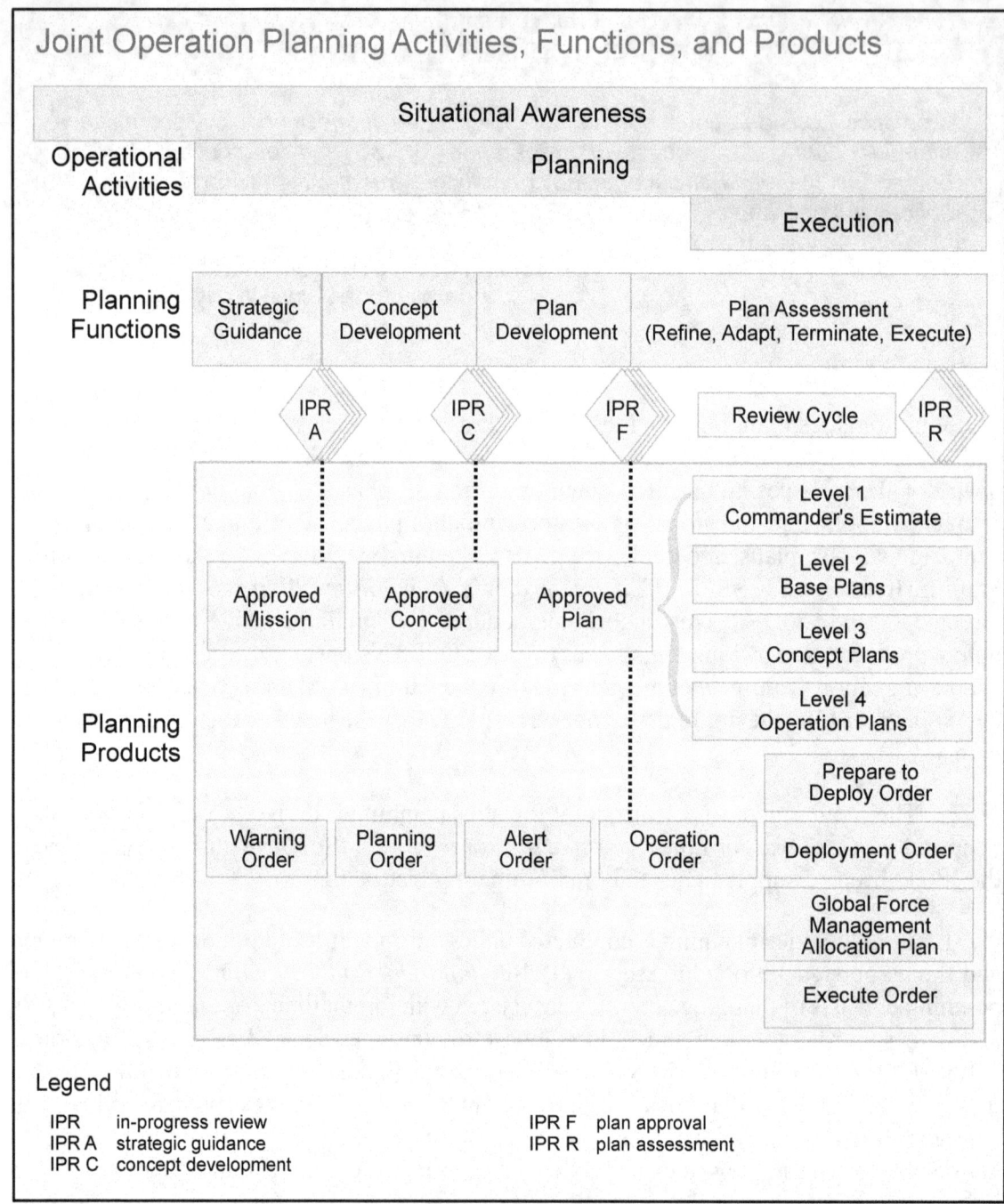

Figure IV-1. Joint Operation Planning Activities, Functions, and Products

understanding of planning assumptions, considerations, risks, COA, implementing actions, and other key factors. Plans may be rapidly modified throughout their development and execution. This process involves expeditious plan reviews and feedback, which can occur at any time, from SecDef and CJCS. The intent is to give SecDef and the CCDR a mechanism for adapting plans rapidly as the situation dictates.

For additional information on operation planning, refer to JP 5-0, Joint Operation Planning.

b. Figure IV-1 portrays the joint operation planning activities, functions, and products. A detailed explanation of each step is found in JP 5-0, *Joint Operation Planning*. This figure provides summary level information applied to the logistics planning process, which the following elements of this chapter will address. Key joint operation planning activities across the planning process are the in-progress reviews (IPRs). IPRs are a disciplined dialogue among strategic leaders discussing the shaping of the plan during development. Logistics core functions and their use, availability and readiness will be addressed in the IPR process as appropriate.

(1) **IPR-A: Strategic Guidance.** The primary end product of the strategic guidance function and IPR A product is an approved CCDR's mission statement for contingency planning and a commander's assessment (operational report-3 pinnacle command assessment) or commander's estimate for crisis action planning.

(2) **IPR-C: Concept Development**

(a) During concept development, the approved mission statement, preliminary COAs, and staff estimates are prepared, then compared, and the CCDR recommends a COA for SecDef approval in the commander's estimate. The SecDef's approved COA from IPR-C is the basis for CONOPS.

(b) Plan development solidifies the CONOPS and the OPLAN, concept plan (CONPLAN), or OPORD and required supporting documents are prepared.

(3) **IPR-F: Plan Approval**

(4) **IPR-R: Plan Review.** The joint planning and execution community does periodic reviews to provide an assessment of the strategic situation and ongoing planning efforts.

c. Using the JOPP framework for deliberate and crisis action planning, Figure IV-2 reflects the cascading relationship from strategic guidance and tasking to planning and developing OPORDs with a focus on TCP and associated key logistics area products. These key logistics area products, TLO, logistics estimate, and concept of logistic support (COLS), support the TCP and provide the basis for deliberate, functional plans, and OPORD development.

d. Figures IV-3 and IV-4 reflect the joint logistics planning process combined with elements of the joint operation planning activities, functions, and products depicted in Figure IV-1. A means of anticipating future requirements is through the theater logistics analysis (TLA) process supporting TLO development and codification, logistics estimate, and logistics planning process. Anticipating requirements is essential to ensuring responsiveness and determining adequacy of support. The purpose of the logistics planning process is to ensure the logistics facts, assumptions, information, and considerations are properly analyzed and effectively synthesized within an integrated plan that supports the CONOPS. To ensure this integration occurs, logistics planners must be included in the planning process as early as possible. The remaining sections of the chapter address process segments and outputs.

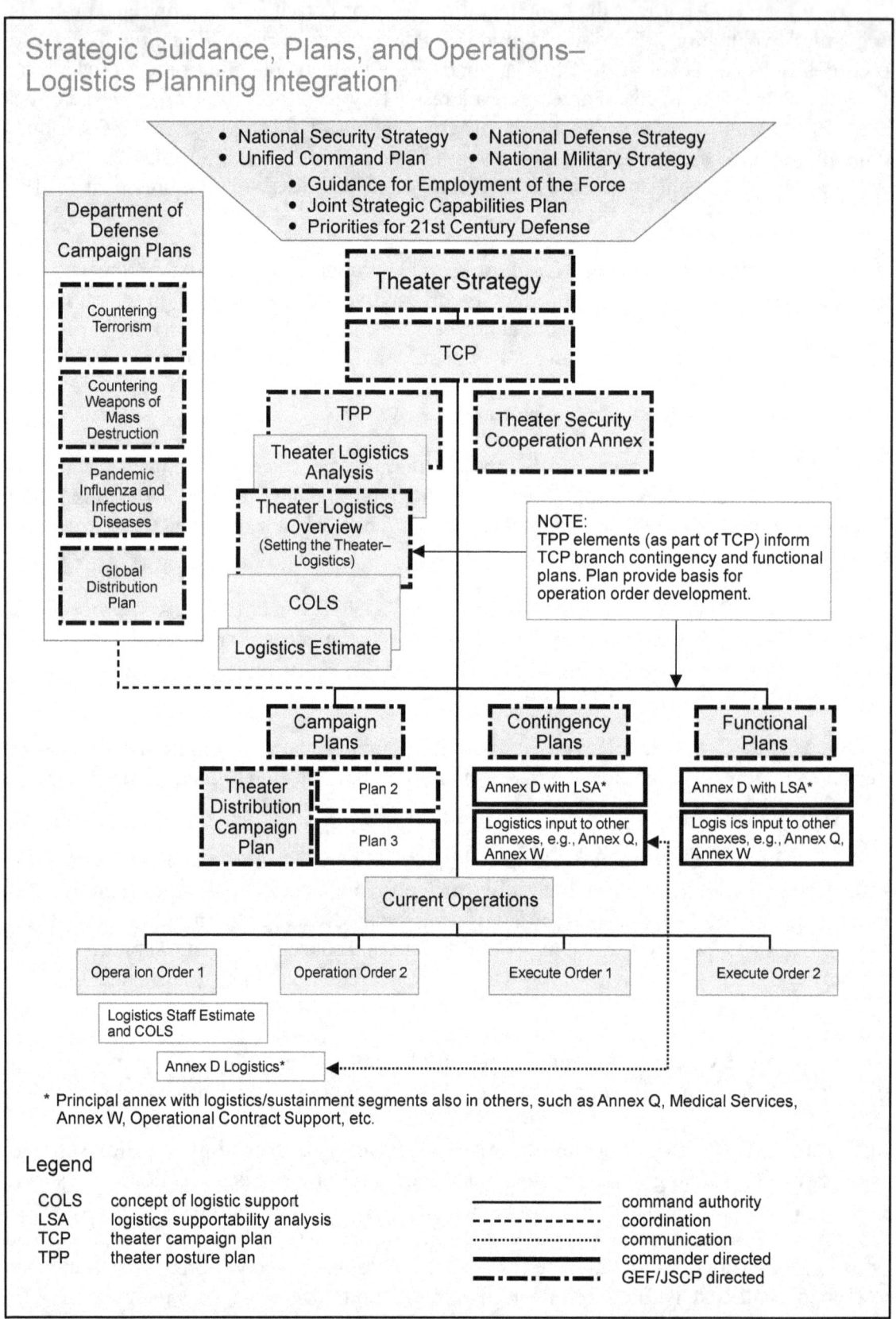

Figure IV-2. Strategic Guidance, Plans, and Operations—Logistics Planning Integration

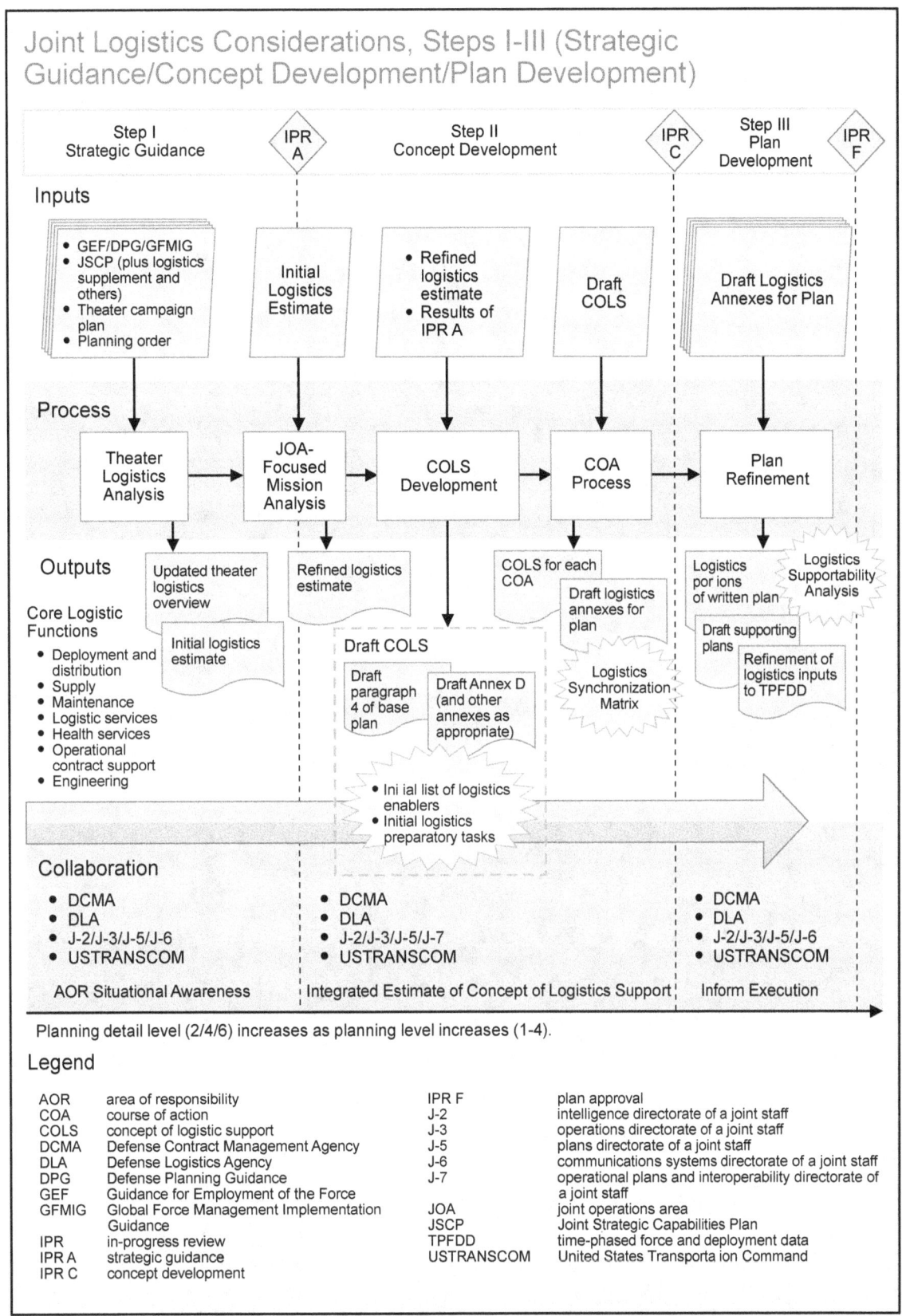

Figure IV-3. Joint Logistics Considerations, Steps I-III (Strategic Guidance/Concept Development/Plan Development)

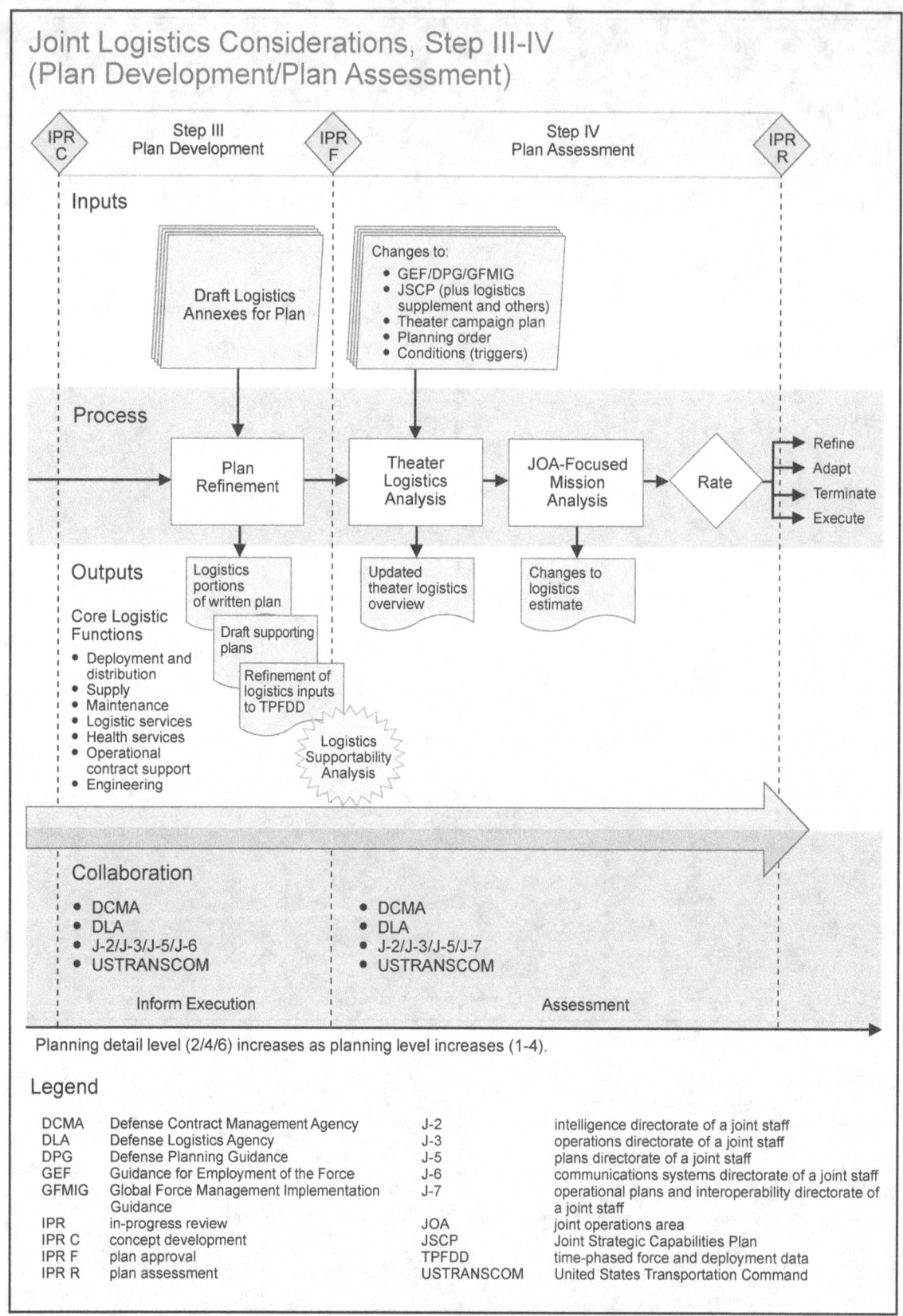

Figure IV-4. Joint Logistics Considerations, Step III-IV (Plan Development/Plan Assessment)

e. **Strategic Guidance.** At the theater level, planning begins with the receipt of strategic guidance or a planning directive and continues as the CCDR develops a mission statement. This planning function relates to the first two JOPP steps: planning initiation and mission analysis. The staffs' planning activities initially focus on mission analysis and developing information to help the commander, staff, and subordinate commanders understand the situation and mission. Planning activities include identifying assumptions, planning forces, mission, and desired end state. Logisticians identify critical logistical assumptions. During mission analysis, joint logisticians must provide critical information to operation planners on the logistics guidance contained in strategic and theater documents. Such documents include the JSCP, JSCP Logistics Supplement, JFC planning guidance, TLA, and TLO. Additionally, detailed information on airfields, seaports, roads, rails, bridging capabilities, and other critical infrastructure captured in the theater posture plan and theater distribution plan are validated and incorporated into the planning efforts.

f. **Concept Development**

(1) This planning function includes the following JOPP steps: COA development, COA analysis and wargaming, COA comparison, and COA approval. The staff, in coordination with supporting commands, Services, and agencies develops, analyzes, and compares valid COAs and prepares staff estimates. The output is an approved COA. Critical elements include a common understanding of the situation, interagency coordination requirements, multinational involvement (if applicable), and capability requirements. Logistics planners must integrate planning efforts with operation planners as deployment, redeployment, distribution, and sustainment requirements are an integral part of COA development. The logistician identifies requirements, critical items, and services needed. They must be aware of force structure planning, TPFDD development, and JRSOI requirements. The logistician uses this planning data during concept of support development to meet sustainment requirements from theater entry and operations to redeployment and reset. Logistics planners address all the core joint logistics functions.

(2) During COA refinement, phasing of joint operations is done to ensure joint capabilities are available in the proper sequence to meet the operational requirements. Events drive phase changes, not time. Phasing helps the planning community visualize the entire operation to define requirements in terms of forces, resources, time, space, and purpose. The planning process uses a standard phasing construct of six phases numbered from 0 to V as depicted in Figure IV-5; however, the CCDR determines the number and nature of the phases during the operational design. Transitions between phases are designed to be distinct shifts in joint force focus and may be accompanied by changes in command relationships. Phase transition often changes priorities, command relationships, force allocation, or even the design of the operational area, thereby creating new support challenges.

(a) Activities in phase 0 focus on shaping the operational environment to support the CCDR's overall objectives and strategic end states. Engagement activities occur during shaping operations, seeking to improve cooperation with allies and other partners. These activities complement broad diplomatic and economic engagement in support of a friendly government's own security activities and setting the theater for major combat

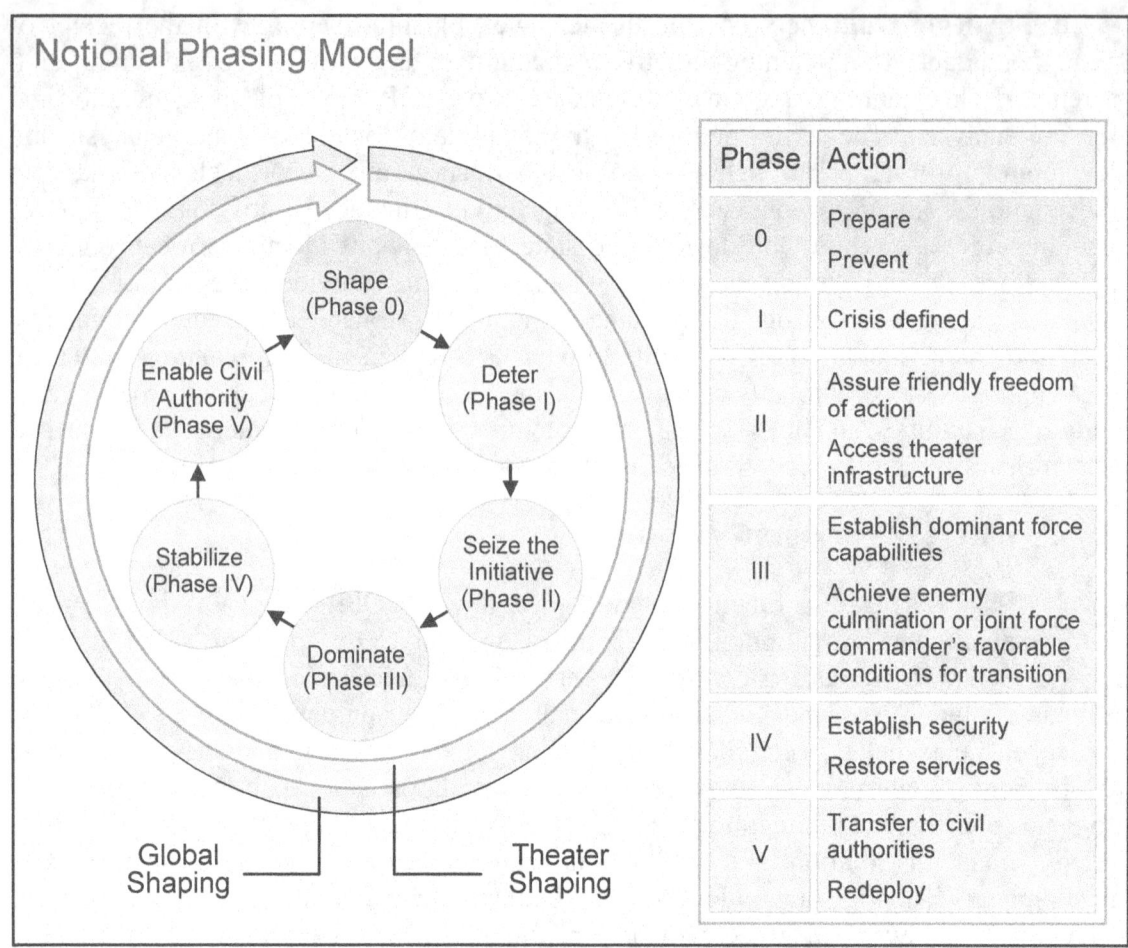

Figure IV-5. Notional Phasing Model

operations. Engagement activity may also occur with new emerging governments and those previously considered as non-friendly to US national interests. SOF are normally highly engaged during phase 0 operations. Joint logistics planners must be aware of SOF requirements during this phase. SOF logistics support includes the sustainment and replenishment of all classes of supply, maintenance, transportation, HS, facilities, BOS, and services. Logistics support of SOF units is the responsibility of the parent Service, except where otherwise provided for by support agreements and/or directives. This may include Service support, joint in-theater support, nonstandard support, special operations-peculiar support. Phase 0 offers logisticians the opportunity to expand knowledge of and access to additional capabilities in anticipation of future events. If it becomes apparent that an event will occur, the logistician can begin preliminary actions, such as pre-positioning of materiel, preparing to surge capabilities, and readying the assets to move on short notice. Phase 0 is a critical period to identify potential risks in terms of access, capabilities, and capacities so alternatives and mitigating measures can be developed. During phase 0, planners must identify and assess critical infrastructure and installation needs and compare the results to current and programmed military construction requirements and authorities. Analysis of required logistics support for deployment and sustainment of flexible deterrent options may occur during this phase.

(b) During phases I and II (Deter and Seize Initiative), the focus is often on preparation for and deployment of forces, rapid expansion of theater presence through the opening of contingency bases for mission specific purposes (such as intermediate staging bases), and reception, staging, onward movement, and integration. Joint logistics planners facilitate appropriate service and component logistics support to SOF elements already in theater. In these phases, a joint expeditionary capability to rapidly establish and initially operate a POD and support expanding distribution may be required to support the CCDR's operational requirements. Movement of materiel may have already begun and must be monitored to ensure that materiel flow is synchronized to the deployment of forces.

(c) During phase III (Dominate), sustaining combat operations is a priority. A key task is to leverage visibility (and terrain visualization) during rapid and dispersed combat operations to see and respond to changing requirements. Joint logisticians should meter the flow of materiel and logistics capabilities in cadence with the tempo of the operation. Data sharing between the operational forces, support forces, and agencies is critical so logisticians are aware of unexpected requirements and unanticipated demands.

(d) Phase IV (Stabilize), often includes providing basic subsistence to the civilian population and equipping of local security forces. During this phase logistics support frequently expands to meet stabilization requirements including critical infrastructure repair, base camps for specific purposes, and improved theater distribution capabilities. Successful phase IV logistics planning requires coordination with multinational, HN, interagency, IGOs, NGOs, or other agencies. Appropriate funding authorities must be clearly understood during this phase.

(e) Phase V (Enable Civil Authority), often requires planning for simultaneously supporting redeployment, force regeneration, relief operations, community assistance, and logistics support, and possible engagement and mentoring at governmental levels ranging from the ministerial to local civil authority. Redeployment and reset typically begins in phase IV, requiring logisticians to begin the disposition and retrograde tasks associated with force withdrawal. This includes the measured and metered drawdown of materiel and logistics capabilities no longer needed or in response to decreased operating tempo.

g. **Plan Development.** During the plan development function, the CCDR's staff creates a detailed OPLAN, OPORD, or CONPLAN, with required annexes. The supported CCDR, subordinate commanders, supporting commanders, CSAs, and staff conduct a number of different planning activities to include force planning, support planning, deployment planning, redeployment or unit rotation planning, shortfall identification, feasibility analysis, refinement, documentation, plan review and approval, and supporting plan development. Planning activities culminate in training and wargaming exercises to provide feedback on the planned concept of support. The joint logistics concept of support specifies how capabilities will be delivered over time, identifies who is responsible for delivering a capability, and defines the critical logistical tasks necessary to achieve objectives during all phases of the operation. The COLS encompasses joint capabilities of all force capabilities to include multinational, HN, interagency, IGOs, NGOs, DOD contract support personnel, plus Active Component and Reserve Component forces.

h. **Plan Assessment.** The supported commander extends and refines planning, while supporting and subordinate commanders and CSAs complete their support plans. Branch plans and other options may be developed. The CCDR and staff continually evaluate the situation for changes which trigger plan refinement, adaptation, termination, or execution. Additional means of assessing joint logistics planning are LSAs completed as appendix 4 (Logistics Supportability Analysis), annex D (Logistics) during plan development, Service component analysis, joint combat capability assessments-plans assessment, Global Logistic Readiness Dashboard, and Defense Readiness Reporting System assessments.

Guidance for development of an LSA is available in the CJCSI 3110.03, Logistics Supplement to the Joint Strategic Capabilities Plan (JSCP); *and the Chairman of the Joint Chiefs of Staff Manual (CJCSM) 3130.03,* Adaptive Planning and Execution (APEX) Planning Formats and Guidance, *provides the LSA format.*

(1) **Preparation for Execution.** This consists of joint force activities to improve the ability to execute an operation. Preparation includes, but is not limited to, plan refinement, rehearsals, intelligence, surveillance and reconnaissance, coordination, inspections, and movement.

(2) **Modeling, Simulations, and Exercises.** The planning process requires the CCDR to conduct modeling and simulations to test operational concepts. This activity may occur as early as COA development to identify potential risks or impediments to mission success. Conducting modeling/simulations by phase of operation can help identify key tasks, roles and responsibilities, and requirements. Consideration for SOF requirements is best captured in phases 0 and 1.

(3) Rehearsals assess the effectiveness of the concept of support, to familiarize supporting joint forces with the concept, and to provide confidence in the selected concept. Rehearsals help clarify roles and responsibilities that are essential to effectively prepare for execution of an operation. Rehearsals are usually part of JOPP step 4, COA analysis and war gaming activities. Coordination conducted with Service logistics components and supporting commands help identify, understand, and validate the correct measure of effectiveness and measure of performance for the CCMD.

3. Joint Operation Planning Process

a. Joint operation planning is the overarching process that guides CCDRs in developing plans for the employment of military power within the context of national strategic objectives and national military strategy to shape events, meet contingencies, and respond to unforeseen crises. Logisticians provide key inputs, analysis and assessments throughout the process. Logistics input is derived from mission analysis, COA development, analysis, selection, and plan development to include preparation and submission of LSA. Previously completed TLA, TLO (setting the theater-logistics), and COLS prepared for the TCP provide a foundational basis for complementary sections for tasked deliberate plans. This foundation can also assist with transition to OPORD preparation for crisis execution under a plan and/or no-plan scenario.

b. In common application, JOPP proceeds according to planning milestones and other requirements across various levels. The seven steps to JOPP are:

(1) **Planning Initiation.** JOPP begins when an appropriate authority recognizes a potential to employ a military capability in response to a potential or actual crisis. The contingency planning guidance in the GEF and JSCP, with supporting supplements such as logistics and mobilization supplements and related strategic guidance statements, serve as the primary guidance to begin contingency planning.

(2) **Mission Analysis.** The primary purpose of JOPP mission analysis is to understand the problem and the purpose of the operation. This will result in the issuance of appropriate guidance to drive the rest of the planning process. A key output is the logistics staff estimate. The logistics staff estimate identifies factors that may influence the feasibility to provide logistics support to the tentative COAs.

(3) **COA Development.** A COA consists of the following information:

(a) What type of military action will occur?

(b) Why the action is required (purpose)?

(c) Who will lead and take the action lead agent, CSA, HN, multinational, etc.)?

(d) When the action will begin?

(e) Where the action will occur?

(f) How the action will occur (method of employment of forces)?

(g) Determination of supportability by personnel, intelligence, operations, logistics, and communications systems?

(h) Who will deploy?

(i) What equipment will deploy?

(j) What capabilities will deploy?

(4) **COA Analysis and Wargaming.** The commander and staff analyze each tentative COA separately according to the commander's guidance. COA analysis identifies advantages and disadvantages of each proposed friendly COA.

(5) **COA Comparison.** This is an objective process whereby COAs are considered independent from each other. Each COA is evaluated and compared against an established set of criteria from the CCMD. The staff helps the commander identify and select the COA that best accomplishes the mission. The staff supports the commander's decision-making process by clearly portraying the commander's options and recording the results of the process. The staff compares feasible COAs to identify the one with the highest probability

of success against the most likely enemy COA and the most dangerous enemy COA. The goal is to identify and recommend the COA that has the highest probability of success against the enemy COA that is of the most concern to the commander.

(6) **COA Approval.** The staff determines the best COA to recommend to the commander, briefs the commander on the COA comparison, the analysis of wargaming results, and includes additional supporting information.

(7) **Plan or Order Development.** The CJCS, in coordination with the supported and supporting commanders and other members of the Joint Chiefs of Staff, monitors planning activities for plans and orders developed per JOPES and APEX policy guidance. Additionally the CJCS resolves shortfalls when required and reviews the supported commander's OPLAN for adequacy, feasibility, acceptability, completeness, and compliance with joint doctrine.

4. Planning Levels

JP 5-0, *Joint Operation Planning,* identifies four levels of planning and establishes a minimum level of effort for each. The supported CCDR may increase the level of effort as necessary.

a. **Level 1 Plan—Commander's Estimate.** This plan requires the development of a COA. The resulting product can be a COA briefing, a commander's estimate or concept, a command directive, or a memorandum—as agreed upon by the CCDR and SecDef.

b. **Level 2 Plan—Base Plan.** This plan culminates in a base plan without annexes (unless otherwise specified) that the CCDR briefs to SecDef at an IPR. Level 2 plans provide sufficient detail to describe the CONOPS, major forces, concepts of support, and anticipated timelines for completing the mission. Unless the CCDR opts to produce an annex D, or the JSCP requires an annex D, there will be an "Administrative and Logistics" section (Paragraph 4) only within the base plan summary.

c. **Level 3 Plan—CONPLAN.** This level is an abbreviated OPLAN with selected annexes and a CCDR's estimate of the plan's feasibility with respect to forces, logistics, and transportation. It will produce, if applicable, a COLS to include a "gross-transportation-feasible" TPFDD, thus, the further delineation of a level 3T plan (i.e., a level three plan with TPFDD). The COLS for Level 3 or 3T plans will mirror the level of detail contained in the supported annex D.

d. **Level 4 Plan—OPLAN.** This plan requires a full description of the CONOPS, a complete set of annexes, and detailed TPFDD. Figure IV-6 depicts logistics planning products by level of plan. Within JOPP, supporting both deliberate and crisis action planning, key logistics outputs are OPORD TLO; logistics estimate supporting development of the commander's estimate and COLS. The COLS further supports annex D for deliberate plans and OPORDs. Appendix 4 to annex D for deliberate plans provides the LSA for the plan. In terms of operations execution, logistics supportability is addressed and status update reported in the JFC's situation report (SITREP) per CJCSM 3150.5, *Joint Reporting System Situation Monitoring Manual.* Logistics input to the

Likely Expected Logistics Outputs

Plan Level	IPR A	IPR C	IPR F	IPR R
Level 1 "Commander's Estimate"	TLO, ILE, and RLE (briefing)			Δs to TLO and RLE (briefing)
Level 2 Base Plan	TLO, ILE, and RLE (briefing)	Paragraph 4 (written and briefing)		Δs to TLO and RLE (briefing)
Level 3 Base Plan with Select Annexes	TLO, ILE, and RLE (briefing)	Paragraph 4, Annex D, logistics enablers, preparation tasks, COLS, and LSM (written and briefing)		Δs to TLO and RLE (briefing)
Level 3 with TPFDD		Transportation feasible TPFDD		
Level 4 Base Plan with Annexes and Detailed TPFDD	TLO, ILE, and RLE (briefing)	Paragraph 4, Annex D, logistics enablers, preparation tasks, COLS, and LSM (written and briefing)	Logistics portions of plan, draft supporting plans, logistics inputs to TPFDD, and LSA (written and briefing)	Δs to TLO, RLE, COLS, and LSA; status of supporting plans (briefing)

Legend

Δ	changes		LSA	logistics supportability analysis
COLS	concept of logistic support		LSM	logistics synchronization matrix
ILE	initial logistics estimate		RLE	refined logistics estimate
IPR	in-progress review		TLO	theater logistics overview
IPR A	strategic guidance		TPFDD	time-phased force and deployment data
IPR C	concept development			
IPR F	plan approval			
IPR R	plan assessment			

Figure IV-6. Likely Expected Logistics Outputs

SITREP assists in providing shared situational awareness and visibility within and across echelons of command to address the core logistics functions, force and sustainment tracking, JRSOI supporting declaration of force closure for operational employment, and other conditions that increase, or materially detract from, the adaptability and readiness of forces. The following paragraphs address key logistics planning process outputs supporting and/or included in TCP development and execution planning.

5. Theater Logistics Analysis

The TLA is a supporting process facilitating development of the TLO through examination, assessment, and codification of an understanding of current conditions of the operational environment. Analysis determines infrastructure, logistics assets/resources, and environmental factors in the operational environment that will optimize or adversely impact means for supporting and sustaining operations (Phase 0 to Phase V). To facilitate developing the TLA, logistic planners leverage all phase 0 interactions with PN logistics professional counterparts (e.g., during multinational exercises logistic planning and execution) to capture insights into their capabilities, processes, and policies by writing and distributing detailed after action reports. The TLA provides a rough detailed country by country analysis of key infrastructure by location or installation (main operating base/forward operating site/cooperative security location); footprint projections; and HN agreements required to support logistically theater peacetime through contingency operations. Work completed supports TLO development as a segment of the TCP and development of directed deliberate/functional plans and OPORDs. Information and data collected and codified during the TLA process are the basis for analysis which assists in identifying, resolving, and/or mitigating risk associated with theater phase 0-phase V operations. The TLA provides the framework for conceptual planning which involves understanding the operational environment and the problem, determining the operation's end state, and visualizing an operational approach. Using the TLA, the operational approach is initially addressed in a logistics estimate and transitions to culminate in the TLO. Detailed planning works out the scheduling, coordination, or technical problems involved with moving, sustaining, and synchronizing the actions of force as a whole toward a common goal. Effective planning requires the integration of both the conceptual and detailed components of planning. The TLA assists in improving the JFC's situational awareness and understanding of theater logistics support capabilities and readiness to support/execute theater operations.

6. Theater Logistics Overview

Development of the TLO is a segment of the iterative planning process which addresses identification, understanding, and framing the theater's overarching mission at the campaign level and uses the TLA combined with elements of operational art to conceive and construct a logistics support approach identified for theater phase 0 to phase V operations. Having captured influencing elements in the TLA as a frame, the JFC's logistics staff elements develop and codify an overarching approach to theater operations in the TLO. The TLO then serves as an important link between conceptual planning and the detailed planning tasked in the GEF/JSCP. The TLO helps the JFC and operations and logistics staff segments measure the overall effectiveness of employing forces, force sustainability, and logistics capability readiness to ensure that the operational approach remains feasible and acceptable. As such, the TLO is key to help identify and address capability gaps, mitigations, and risk. If risk cannot be resolved or mitigated to an acceptable level then the operational concept may be reframed. Reframing involves revisiting earlier COAs, conclusions, and decisions that underpin the current operational CONOPS. Reframing can lead to a modification of the current CONOPS or result in preparation of a branch plan or entirely new plan. In developing the TLO, logistics planners in coordination with intelligence and operations staff segments identify opportunities/initiatives by anticipating events allowing them to identify decision points to operate inside the threat's decision cycle, or to react promptly to deteriorating situation advancing beyond phase 0 operations. Time to complete the TLA and resulting TLO assists in optimizing available planning time for associated detailed plan tasks. Based on their understanding and learning gained during TLO development, the JFC and senior logistics staff representative issue logistics planning guidance to support and enable the operational approach expressed in the CONOPS and to guide more detailed planning. The TLO is a key component to establish a common frame of reference to develop plans/OPORDs, prepare for, execute, and assess operations. See Appendix A, "Theater Logistics Overview Format," for an example of a TLO format.

7. Logistics Estimate

Logistics estimate supports the commander's estimate, COLS, OPORD development, and execution. Execution planning may involve abbreviated and compressed timelines from situational awareness/initiating event and reporting to potential JFC planning guidance or CJCS planning order to OPORD and execution. The TLA and TLO provide a foundation for rapid review and response development. Due to accelerated timelines, availability, and incorporation of TLA information and TLO segments, preparation of the logistics estimate may be compressed supporting the commander's estimate and initial work for COA development, analysis, and selection. Updating the TLA/TLO baseline, the logistics estimate supporting the commander's estimate supports the COLS prepared for OPORD annex D development and iterative planning during operations execution. The logistics estimate is an analysis of how CSS factors can affect mission accomplishment. It contains the logistics staff's comparison of requirements and capabilities, conclusions, and recommendations about the feasibility of supporting a specified COA. This estimate includes how the core logistics functions affect various COA(s). Preparation of the logistics estimate provides a coordinated and formalized means for the staff to identify and consider logistics shaping in support of the operational CONOPS. The logistics effort and development of the logistics estimate refined as COLS for OPORD annex D must be integrated into the joint operational planning process and OPORD development upfront. Using the TLA/TLO baseline, logistics staff segments will be able to identify if specific operational actions to augment or expand theater logistics capabilities to support the operational CONOPS must be taken. The previously developed TLA/TLO assists the logistics planners in providing logistic characteristics of the AOR and area of operations/area of interest for the specified operations. The TLA/TLO aids crisis planners in identification of logistics infrastructure of the operational environment (what exists in the battlefield that may be put to use). See Appendix B, "Logistics Staff Estimate Format," for an example format.

8. Concept of Logistic Support

In support of the CCDR and preparation of deliberate plans/OPORDs, the logistics staff elements prepare a logistics estimate which is further refined and developed into a COLS. The COLS provides a foundational basis in preparation of annex D for assigned contingency plans and/or OPORD development tasks. The COLS establishes priorities of support across all phases of operations to support the JFC's CONOPS. Logistics staff elements' active participation within and across JOPP process activities at all echelons facilitates CONOPS and associated COLS development. A COLS addresses the sustainment of forces to include identification and status of theater support bases, intermediate staging bases, forward staging bases, and assignment of contingency base operation responsibilities. (The CCDR may assign a component commander with the responsibility for conducting base support at designated theater bases by exercising DAFL); afloat assets; identification and status of theater sustainment elements to include identification and/or forecast of required augmentation; priority of sustainment by class of supply with guidance on days of supply to be maintained (minimum and maximum); movement priorities for airlift and sealift aligned to JFC's CONOPS; guidance for employment of sea-air interfaces to facilitate JRSOI; controlling CUL; JFC's declaration of force closure; actions by phase (phase 0-phase V); and logistics assets required.

For more information on the COLS, see CJCSI 3110.03, Logistics Supplement to the Joint Strategic Capabilities Plan (JSCP).

9. Transition to Execution

Planning does not cease with development, submission and approval of a plan or OPORD. Planning is iterative and continues throughout as actions and assessments evolve in a dynamic manner across command echelons from the strategic national to operational to tactical levels. Strategic guidance for plans as well as plan segments and resulting OPORDs is refined as situational awareness and understanding evolves. Through assessment, guidance and/or plans may be reframed. Assessment is a determination of the progress toward accomplishing a task, creating an effect, or achieving an objective. Assessment is a continuous activity to support the operation process and associated planning and execution activities. During planning, assessment focuses on understanding current conditions of an operational environment and assumptions to address mission, enemy, terrain and weather, troops and support available, time available, and civil considerations. During preparation, assessment focuses on determining force readiness to execute the operation and verifying the assumptions on which the plan is based. During execution, assessment focuses on evaluating progress of the operation. Based on their assessments, commanders at various echelons direct adjustment to the plan/OPORD ensuring the plan/OPORD/operation stays focused on mission.

CHAPTER V
EXECUTING JOINT LOGISTICS

> *"You will not find it difficult to prove that battles, campaigns, and even wars have been won or lost primarily because of logistics."*
>
> **General Dwight D. Eisenhower, US Army (1890-1969)**

1. Introduction

The term "executing joint logistics" is used to describe actions and operations conducted by joint logistics forces in support of the JFC mission. Force reception, theater distribution, and MA are examples of joint logistics operations. Since joint logistics operations span the strategic, operational, and tactical levels, the transition from planning to execution is critical.

2. Joint Logistics Execution

JFCs adapt to evolving mission requirements and operate effectively across a range of military operations. These operations differ in complexity and duration. The joint logistician must be aware of the characteristics and focus of these operations and tailor logistics support appropriately. This range of military operations extends from shaping activities to major operations and campaigns. US and multinational partners collaborate to expand mutual support and leverage capabilities to quickly respond to future contingencies.

   a. **Military Engagement, Security Cooperation, and Deterrence.** The GEF directs development of TCPs focused on current operations, military engagement, security cooperation, and other shaping or preventative activities. Shaping activities include military engagement, security cooperation, and deterrence. Developing mutually supportive relationships to enhance coordination is an important enabler for joint logistics operations. Acquisition and cross-servicing agreements (ACSAs) are bilateral international agreements that allow for the provision of cooperative logistics support under the authority granted in Title 10, USC, Sections 2341-2350. They are governed by DODD 2010.9, *Acquisition and Cross-Servicing Agreements,* and implemented by CJCSI 2120.01, *Acquisition and Cross-Servicing Agreements.* ACSAs are intended to provide an alternative acquisition option for logistics support in support of exercises or exigencies. Effective joint and multinational logistics operations in phase 0 provide the foundation for an expanded role in later crises while providing additional warfighting capability. Specific issues that can be addressed in phase 0 include securing interagency approvals; addressing PN and regional sensitivities, changing politics and overall stability; determining optimal presence and posture; BPC; and developing formal agreements/permissions between the US and PNs.

      (1) The above issues play heavily on where and when DOD can secure permissions for events and support. PNs often need extended timelines before they are prepared to permit additional bilateral or multilateral events. Additionally, positive US relations and successful bilateral engagement in one nation can impact US interests in other regional locations. Successful execution of bilateral events does not guarantee continued access.

(2) **Determining Optimal Presence and Posture.** Persistent DOD presence in other nations is often not desired by country teams or PN governments. Maintaining a low visibility signature of US DOD presence and activities often assists in obtaining future interagency and PN permissions. In some instances, interagency and PN mandates not only limit US military presence, but also affect US civilian contractors. In these instances, logistics support or construction must be executed through local nationals or third-country nationals.

(3) Formal agreements and permissions between the US and developing nations often involve long approval processes and restrictions on the types of funding and support authorized.

b. **Crisis Response and Limited Contingency Operations.** US military history indicates crisis response and limited contingency operations are typically single, small-scale, limited-duration operations. Many of these operations involve a combination of military forces and capabilities in close cooperation with other government agencies, IGOs, and NGOs. Logisticians must understand multinational and interagency logistics capabilities and coordinate mutual support, integrating them into the joint operation when appropriate. Efforts during shaping operations to develop partner capacities can pay dividends in these types of operations. Many crisis response missions, such as foreign humanitarian assistance and disaster relief operations, require time-sensitive sourcing of critical commodities and capabilities, and rapid delivery to the point of need. In these operations, joint logistics is often the main effort, often operating in support of the Department of State. Defense support of civil authorities refers to the unique DOD ability to provide support to civil authorities. DOD responds to requests for support to civilian authorities under the National Response Framework in order to save lives, protect the environment, and mitigate human suffering under imminently serious conditions.

For additional information see JP 3-28, Defense Support of Civil Authorities, *and JP 3-41,* Chemical, Biological, Radiological, and Nuclear Consequence Management.

c. **Major Operations or Campaigns.** Major operations or campaigns typically involve the deployment, sustainment, redeployment, and retrograde of large combat forces. Joint logistics can be executed by an appointed lead Service or agency for common user logistics. Joint logisticians develop support plans for the duration of the operation, as well as the return of personnel and equipment to the continental United States or other locations. These plans often leverage contractor support to augment Service logistics capabilities. The primary challenges for logisticians during these types of operations are identifying the requirements, ensuring logistics issues are considered among competing priorities, and adjusting to the situation to ensure sustained readiness and synchronized timelines as the operation transitions across phases. A critical planning requirement during major operations is to plan for the transition to phase IV (Stabilize), and phase V (Enable Civil Authority), where logisticians will have competing requirements to support stability operations, provide basic services and foreign humanitarian assistance, and assist with reconstruction efforts, while redeploying forces and equipment. The retrograde of contaminated materiel will require special handling to control contamination and protect the force and mission resources. Demilitarization and disposition of material and equipment will also require significant planning to ensure these missions are successfully conducted.

For operations incorporating CWMD, see JP 3-40, Countering Weapons of Mass Destruction.

3. Essential Elements for Joint Logistics Execution

a. **Organizing for Execution.** The CCMD J-4 is responsible for an effective transition of logistics operations from peacetime or planning activities to monitoring, assessing, planning, and directing logistics operations throughout the theater. This transition may occur through the directed expansion of the JLOC and/or the CCDR's JDDOC. The CCDR's or JFC's staff is augmented (either physically or virtually) with representatives from Service components, USTRANSCOM and other supporting CCDRs, CSAs, and other national partners or agencies outside the command's staff. For example, each GCC has established a JDDOC to synchronize and optimize the flow of arriving forces and materiel between the intertheater and intratheater transportation. As the operating tempo increases during a contingency or crisis, additional joint logisticians and selected subject matter experts (e.g., maintenance, ordnance, supply) can augment JDDOCs and use established networks and command relationships instead of creating new staffs with inherent startup delays and inefficiencies. This expanded organization must be organized and situated to ensure increased coordination and synchronization of requirements in the deployment and distribution process. This organization must have clear roles and responsibilities between the various elements and clearly understood relationships between the logistics elements and the CCMD staff.

b. **Visibility and Technology.** Logisticians use a variety of automated tools to assist in planning and execution.

Troops embark on a combat logistics patrol to take supplies to Marines and Sailors with Regimental Combat Team 8 and 1st Battalion, 8th Marine Regiment, 1st Marine Division (Forward) in Afghanistan.

See Chapter III, "Coordinating and Synchronizing Joint Logistics," for more information on technology.

c. **Achieving Situational Awareness.** A role of the joint logistician is to support the JFC in achieving situational awareness in order to make decisions and disseminate and execute directives. Maintaining situational awareness requires maintaining visibility over the status and location of resources, over the current and future requirements of the force, and over the joint and component processes that deliver support to the joint force. In order to provide this visibility, timely and accurate data and information are required for all equipment, sustaining supplies, repair parts, munitions, fuel and etc., moving into, within, exiting, being stored, or stored in the GCC's AOR. This kind of visibility is the key to continuously monitoring progress and is enabled by operational inputs which serve to inform joint logisticians about the current situation. Service reports, operational summaries, and logistics situation reports all serve to expand the joint logistician's awareness of the JOA. Awareness is enhanced through automated systems and reports such as the munitions report and bulk petroleum contingency report. JFCs can use this information to develop a logistics dimension to the JFC's overall situational awareness. This logistics information should be updated on a continuous basis through the use of information technology and available joint decision support and visualization tools such as GCSS-J. Collectively this information enables joint logisticians to assess planned versus actual consumption in order to detect possible shortfalls, predict requirements, and develop possible solutions to issues. This data should be used to anticipate requirements and capabilities near-term (10 days or less), mid-term (about 30 days), or long-term (beyond 30 days).

d. **Battle Rhythm.** The CCDR will establish a battle rhythm for the operation along with mechanisms for establishing and maintaining visibility for all functional areas, to include logistics. The joint logistician must develop a supporting battle rhythm for the sustainment staff that supports the JFC battle rhythm and is designed to provide the JFC with proactive logistic options. Synchronizing logistics reporting with operational updates, ensuring that the operational planning cycle is part of the logistics battle rhythm, and minimizing shift changes at critical points in the battle rhythm will enable more effective execution. Additionally, tying the component logistics elements to the JFC's battle rhythm will provide more accurate and timely situational awareness and promote better integrated support to the joint force.

e. **Joint Logistics Boards, Offices, Centers, Cells, and Groups.** The joint logistician will often use boards, centers, or other organizations to assist the J-4 staff in executing joint logistics operations, by prioritizing and/or allocating resources, controlling functions or prioritizing requirements.

More information about these organizations can be found in Appendix C, "Joint Logistics Staff Organizations."

f. **Execution Synchronization.** A synchronization matrix or decision support tool/template can establish common reference points to help assess the progress of an operation. Joint logisticians may use a matrix to display progress against actual execution and recommend adjustments as needed. A logistics synchronization matrix is built around the concept of the operation, and normally contains the phasing of the operation over time along the horizontal axis. The vertical axis normally contains the functions the joint logistician integrates into a concept of support. The body of the matrix contains the critical tasks, arrayed in time and linked to responsible elements for execution. This decision support tool enables logisticians to graphically display the logistics concept of support, see potential gaps, develop options to mitigate those gaps, and respond to a changing operational environment.

g. **Commander's Critical Information Requirements (CCIRs).** CCIRs are elements of friendly and enemy information the commander identifies as critical to timely decision making. Joint logisticians update the critical information requirements related to logistics. Joint logisticians will most often use friendly forces information requirements to guide decision making. Those requirements are often a direct reflection of resources (force availability, unit readiness, or materiel availability).

4. Terminating Joint Operations

Terminating joint operations is an aspect of the CCDR's strategy that links to achievement of national strategic objectives. The supported CCDR can develop and propose specified conditions approved by the President or SecDef that must be met before a joint operation can be concluded. These termination criteria help define the desired military end state, which normally represents a period in time or set of conditions beyond which the President does not require the military instrument of national power as the primary means to achieve remaining national objectives.

For additional information, see JP 3-0, Joint Operations.

a. **Concluding Joint Logistics Operations.** Joint logistics operations are always ongoing, but it is possible that some aspects of logistic operations could be completed before the operation has concluded. For example, force reception operations could be completed when forces have been placed under the control of the commander for integration and employment, and no other forces are flowing into the JOA. Joint logisticians monitor transitional activities and ensure resources are fully utilized or redeployed. Withdrawal and redeployment from an operation are challenging and require a synchronized and holistic effort by joint logisticians. Maintenance support planning should address the process for determining equipment disposition, and the requirements for preparing equipment for shipment. In addition, maintenance support planning should ensure that equipment is available for movement when required while minimizing the impact on readiness. In accordance with DOD policies, logisticians plan for the disposition of materiel, such as retrograde and demilitarization, scrap removal, and disposal of hazardous waste and when required, clearance decontamination of supplies and equipment.

b. **Theater Closure.** When it has been determined that joint operations should be terminated, joint logistic operations focus tasks that include redeploying personnel and materiel from the JOA to a new operational area or home station/demobilization station; transitioning materiel to HN; foreign military sales; or disposal of materiel. Joint logistics operations also play a major role in closing ports to military operations and terminating operational contracts and agreements.

Intentionally Blank

APPENDIX A
THEATER LOGISTICS OVERVIEW FORMAT

1. (U) Situation

Commander, USEXAMPLECOM has directed the development of USEXAMPLECOM Campaign Plan. The intent of USEXAMPLECOM Campaign Plan is to provide linkages between strategic/national level assets/enablers. This TLO identifies the theater logistics capabilities and shortfalls as they specifically affect the USEXAMPLECOM AOR.

2. (U) Host-Nation Support and Logistics Support Agreements

Identify and address host-nation support (HNS) and logistics support agreement that should be included in all logistics support plans relating to AOR contingencies. Identify and address applicable agreements per format examples below.

a. (U) **Wartime Host-Nation Support (WHNS) Program with the XXX.** This program is covered XXXX updated day/month/year. WHNS is defined as (HN) provided military or civilian resources and assistance for the reception, staging, onward movement, and sustainment of US forces in times of crisis, hostilities, or war. The WHNS program contains technical arrangements for support in the following areas: communications, engineering, field services, maintenance, medical, munitions, CBRN services, personnel and labor services, petroleum, security, supply and transportation. Requirements are updated within the WHNS program every two years, and the approved WHNS assets are reflected in the provisional WHNS support plan.

b. (U) **ACSA with XXX.** Identify and address all individual agreements between the US and the HN that are legal agreements with the HN in which the US agrees to provide logistics support, supplies, and services (LSS) to military force of a qualifying country organization in return for the reciprocal provision of LSS by such government or organization to elements of the United States Armed Forces. A cross-servicing agreement may also be referred to as a mutual logistics support agreement.

c. (U) **Shipping and/or Airlift Support Agreements.** Identify and address individual agreement.

d. (U) **Petroleum Agreement with XXX.** Identify and address individual agreement.

3. (U) Strategic Air and Sea Ports of Debarkation

This section will discuss the current capacity/capability at these AOR air and sea port locations and existing issues. Identify the source of information as well as currently known long-term gaps. Identify and address air and seaports below:

a. (U) **Strategic Air Ports of Debarkation in the XXX**

(1) (U) Aaaa Airfield.

(2) (U) Bbbb Airfield.

(3) (U) Cccc Air Base.

(4) (U) Dddd Air Base.

b. (U) **Strategic Sea Ports of Debarkation in the XXX**

(1) (U) Aaaa Port.

(2) (U) Bbbb Port.

(3) (U) Cccc Port.

(4) (U) Dddd Ammo Port.

c. (U) **Strategic Air Ports of Debarkation in XXX**

(1) (U) Aaaa Airfield.

(2) (U) Bbbb Airfield.

(3) (U) Cccc IAP.

d. (U) **Strategic Sea Ports of Debarkation in XXX**

(1) (U) Aaaa Port.

(2) (U) Bbbb Pier.

(3) (U) Cccc Dock.

(4) (U) Dddd Port.

e. (U) **Strategic Air Ports of Debarkation in XXX**

(1) (U) Aaaa IAP.

(2) (U) Bbbb IAP.

f. (U) **Strategic Sea Ports of Debarkation in XXX**

(1) (U) Aaaa Port.

(2) (U) Bbbb Harbor.

g. (U) **Other Strategic Distribution Nodes Required to Support Contingencies in the AOR**

(1) (U) Aaaa Ocean Terminal.

(2) (U) Bbbb Port.

(3) (U) Cccc Ocean Terminal.

4. (U) Pre-Positioned and Theater Reserve Stocks

Address afloat pre-positioned war reserve materiel (PWRM) and/or shore based PWRM within the USEXAMPLECOM AOR. Address apportioned assets and use.

    a. (U) Aaaa.

    b. (U) Bbbb.

    c. (U) Cccc.

5. (U) Joint Logistic Functions

Address CS and CSS capabilities within and across the AOR which may vary by location and command. Provide a CS and CSS capabilities overview within the AOR by logistics capability area. Description of core logistic functions should be addressed as a minimum, per guideline description below:

    a. (U) **Deployment and Distribution.** Provide an overview of current theater capabilities that addresses control segments of the CCDR's methodology for distribution pipeline control; assesses deployment and distribution networks and capacity aligned to data about the theater distribution infrastructure provided in paragraph 3 above; identify unique assumptions about deployment and distribution operations; and identify peacetime and contingency distribution partners and specify tasks each must provide in terms of peacetime and contingency administrative, logistical, communications, and funding.

    b. (U) **Supply.** Provide theater country assessments that identify supply and service installations and supply stocks available in theater. Address operating stockage objectives and safety levels. Indicate apportioned pre-positioned war reserve materiel to support deployments pending resupply. Specify source and location of starter and swing stocks that will be drawn until normal resupply rates achieved. Specify significant special arrangements required for materiel support beyond the normal supply procedure. Indicate shortfalls/ overages resulting from comparison of requirements and assets estimated to be available.

    c. (U) **Maintenance.** Identify current theater facility capabilities and requirements for maintenance and modification facilities existing and/or needed to support the plan. Indicate the level of maintenance to be performed and where it is to occur, including host-nation or contractor facilities, if applicable. Address theater capabilities for inspection, test, service, repair, rebuild, calibration, and savage.

    d. (U) **Logistic Services.** Aligned to paragraph 2 above, address major support arrangements and contracts with industry or third-party logistics providers that are presently in effect or that will be executed in support of the plan. Include significant inter-Service support arrangements. (Refer to appropriate annexes or appendices within the agreements.)

Services to be addressed include, but not limited to food service; water, water management and ice service; contingency base services; container and 463L pallet management; hygiene services; and MA.

e. (U) **OCS.** Identify OCS applicable to the theater and the policies guiding the activities. Areas of consideration include existing in-theater contracting capability, control and supporting constructs, contracting COI, augmentation, Synchronized Predeployment Operational Tracker, and locations off key contracting organizations/offices.

f. (U) **Engineering.** Identify and address engineering support capabilities and activities applicable to the theater and the policies for providing these services. Identify and address theater capability to provide installation assets and services necessary to support US military forces through real property life-cycle management and installation services. Assess installation support capability in terms of accessing/gaining control of an installation, maintaining facilities support, and sustaining facilities operations and services within the theater.

g. (U) **HS.** Identify and provide overview all theater medical infrastructures. This is done by identifying appropriate Service, country, capability and readiness of the facility, current and planned military construction requirements, and proposed changes to capabilities at each location including recommendations for maintaining, closing, or enhancing each facility.

6. (U) **Logistics Capability Shortfalls**

Identify and address capability shortfalls and inherit risk(s) and means to resolve or mitigate.

a. (U) Deployment and Distribution.

b. (U) Supply.

c. (U) Maintenance.

d. (U) Logistic Services.

e. (U) OCS.

f. (U) Engineering.

g. (U) HS.

APPENDIX B
LOGISTICS STAFF ESTIMATE FORMAT

Originating Division, Issuing Headquarters
Place of Issue
Date-Time-Group, Month, Year
LOGISTIC ESTIMATE NUMBER _____*
References: (1) JP 4-0, *Joint Logistics.*
                 (2) JP 5-0, *Joint Operation Planning.*
                 (3) USEXAMPLECOM TLO.
                 (4) Maps and Charts.
                 (5) Other pertinent documents.

1. Mission

State the mission of the command as a whole, taken from the commander's mission analysis, planning guidance, or other statements.

2. Situation and Considerations

   a. **Characteristics of the Area of Operations.** Summarize data about the area, taken from the intelligence estimate or area study, with specific emphasis on significant factors affecting logistics activities.

   b. **Enemy Forces**

      (1) **Strength and Disposition.** Refer to current intelligence estimate.

      (2) **Enemy Capabilities.** As analyzed and evaluated within the joint intelligence preparation of the operational environment process, discuss enemy capabilities, taken from current intelligence estimates, with specific emphasis on their impact on the logistics situation. Describe enemy abilities to interdict strategic sealift and airlift, to attack and reduce the effectiveness of transportation nodes, and to attack pre-positioned stocks ashore and afloat, if applicable.

   c. **Friendly Forces**

      (1) **Present Disposition of Major Elements.** Include estimates of their strengths.

      (2) **Own COAs.** State the proposed COAs under consideration, obtained from operations or plans division.

   d. **Probable Tactical Developments.** Review major deployments and logistics preparations necessary in all phases of the operation proposed.

   e. **Logistics Unit Status.** State known personnel problems, if any, that may affect the logistics situation.

f. **Assumptions.** State assumptions about the logistics aspects of the situation made for this estimate. Because basic assumptions for the operation already have been made and will appear in planning guidance and in the plan itself, they should not be repeated here. Certain logistics assumptions may have been made in preparing this estimate, and those should be stated.

g. **Special Features.** Special features not covered elsewhere in the estimate that may influence the logistics situation may be stated here.

h. **Logistics Situation**

(1) **Supply and Service Installations.** Describe and give location of key supply and service installations that will be used to support the operation. State known dry and refrigerated storage capabilities and shortfalls and include COAs to mitigate capability gaps.

(2) **Supply.** State the availability of pre-positioned war reserve stocks, authorized levels of supply, known deficiencies of supply stocks and supply systems, and responsibilities and policies regarding supply.

(3) **Transportation.** List air, sea, and surface transportation availability, coordination, regulations, lift capability, responsibilities, and policies regarding supply.

(4) **HS.** Describe availability of evacuation and hospital facilities and medical responsibilities and policies, including the anticipated evacuation policy.

(5) **OCS.** Describe how contracting supports the operation and articulates the commander's priorities, intent, and specific OCS command guidance by phase of operation. Address the overall contract support arrangements (e.g., support to own Services, lead Service or joint theater support contracting command). As available, identify key contracting, separate CCAS organizations (if applicable) and by unit, operational phase, and location for respectively assigned deployment destinations. As available address estimated numbers of support personnel (i.e., passengers) for each assigned unit. Address locations and/or support relationships, designated support areas of key contracting organizations/offices by phase of operation.

(6) **Engineering Support.** List responsibilities for engineering support, limiting factors, and other appropriate considerations. Refer to the annex D appendix 6 for the full engineer support plan.

(7) **Base and Installation Support.** List responsibilities for base and installation support, limiting factors, and other appropriate considerations.

(8) **Miscellaneous.** Include other logistics matters not considered elsewhere that may influence selection of a specific COA. Include identity of known deficiencies of CSS. Include identity of civil and indigenous materiel resources available or essential to support military operations. Also, consider the requirement to meet minimum essential needs of civil populace for whom the commander may become responsible.

3. Logistic Analysis of Own Courses of Action

Make an orderly examination of logistic considerations for the proposed COAs to determine the manner and degree of that influence. The objective of this analysis is to determine if the logistics requirements can be met and to isolate the logistics implications that should be weighed by the commander in the commander's estimate of the situation.

a. Analyze each COA from the logistics point of view. The detail in which the analysis is made is determined by considering the level of command, scope of contemplated operations, and urgency of need.

b. For each COA under consideration, analyze the logistic functions and concerns described in paragraph 2. Examine these factors realistically from the standpoint of requirements versus actual or programmed capabilities, climate and weather, hydrography, time and space, enemy capabilities, and other significant factors that may have an impact on the logistics situation as it affects the COAs.

c. Throughout the analysis, keep logistics considerations foremost in mind. The analysis is not intended to produce a decision; it is intended to ensure applicable logistic functions have been considered and serve as the basis for comparisons in paragraph 4.

4. Comparison of Own Courses of Action

a. List the advantages and disadvantages of each proposed COA from the J-4's point of view.

b. Use a worksheet similar to that used for the commander's estimate, if necessary.

5. Conclusions

a. State whether or not the mission set forth in paragraph 1 can be supported from a logistics standpoint.

b. State which COA under consideration can best be supported from a logistics standpoint.

c. Identify the major logistics deficiencies that must be brought to the commander's attention. Include recommendations concerning the methods to eliminate or reduce the effects of those deficiencies.

(Signed)
J-4

Intentionally Blank

APPENDIX C
JOINT LOGISTICS STAFF ORGANIZATIONS

1. General

There are a number of logistics boards, centers, and programs that reside at the strategic and operational levels that can be used to resolve joint logistics issues during operations. These enduring or temporary organizations may be staffed on a permanent or full time basis, such as the JLOC at the Joint Staff J-4, or on a temporary basis such as a SAPO at a JTF to resolve specific strategic and operational gaps, shortfalls, or the impact of competition with another supported commander's concurrent operations. These organizations have specified responsibilities and relationships identified in DOD or CJCS issuances and memoranda, or CCMD planning documents.

2. Strategic-Level Joint Logistics Staff Organizations

Strategic-level joint logistics staff organizations provide advice or allocation recommendations to the CJCS concerning prioritizations, allocations, policy modifications or procedural changes.

a. **Joint Logistics Board (JLB).** The JLB provides oversight and forges unity of effort across the logistics community to most effectively meet the JFC's operational requirements. The JLB drives integration and optimization of logistics processes and advocates for logistics capabilities by ensuring a systematic approach, senior leadership review, and approval of joint logistics requirements. The JLB is chaired by ASD(L&MR) and the Joint Staff J-4 and includes representatives from the Services, USTRANSCOM, and DLA.

b. **Joint Materiel Priorities and Allocation Board (JMPAB).** The JMPAB is the organization representing the CJCS in matters that establish materiel priorities or allocate resources. The CJCS, through the JMPAB, establishes, modifies, or recommends policies for allocating materiel assets in the DOD system when competing requirements among DOD components cannot be resolved by those components. The board, when convened, is chaired by the Joint Staff J-4 and includes representatives of the following: J-3, J-5, J-6 [communications system directorate of a joint staff; command, control, communications, and computer systems staff section], J-8 [Joint Staff Directorate for Force Structure, Resource, and Assessment], Service logisticians, DLA, US Special Operations Command (when required), and DSCA (for issues concerning use of a force activity designator, project code, or force module subsystem).

c. **Joint Transportation Board (JTB).** The JTB may be convened by the CJCS during wartime or contingencies to ensure the President and SecDef transportation requirements are apportioned and scheduled. When convened, the JTB adjudicates competing requirements and, when required, evaluates COAs to make recommendations to the CJCS.

For additional information on the JTB, refer to JP 4-01, The Defense Transportation System.

d. **JLOC.** The JLOC is a current operations directorate within the Joint Staff J-4. The JLOC receives reports from supporting commands, Service components, and external sources, distills information for decision/briefings, and responds to questions. The JLOC coordinates and synchronizes the planning and execution of ongoing CCMD operations, interagency support requirements, and validates priority movement for selected senior officials.

e. **Deployment and Distribution Operations Center (DDOC).** The DDOC located at USTRANSCOM directs the global air, land, and sea transportation capabilities of the Defense Transportation System to meet national security objectives provided by DOD. The DDOC fuses capabilities of multimodal deployment and distribution operations, intelligence, force protection, capacity acquisition, resource management, and other staff functions to collaboratively provide distribution options to the warfighter. C2 of the majority of intertheater lift forces and logistics infrastructure is accomplished through the DDOC, which tracks the movement requirement from lift allocation and initial execution through closure at final destination.

For additional information concerning the DDOC, refer to JP 3-35, Deployment and Redeployment Operations.

f. **Defense Health Board (DHB).** The DHB is a federal advisory committee to SecDef. As an independent authoritative advisory body it serves to maximize the health, safety, and effectiveness of US Armed Forces. The DHB provides scientific advice and recommendations pertaining to operational programs, health policy development, and health research programs and requirements for the treatment and prevention of disease and injury. Additionally, it provides counsel for health promotions and health care delivery in support of DOD beneficiaries.

g. **Defense Medical Materiel Program Office (DMMPO).** The DMMPO is an operating entity under the TRICARE Management Activity within FHP and readiness programs. The mission of the DMMPO is to establish clinical, logistics, and program policy, as well as support medical materiel development and acquisition processes across the Military Departments. The DMMPO promotes clinically driven, evidence based, standardization of medical supplies and equipment, efficiency in the acquisition and life cycle management of medical materiel, and joint interoperability of medical capabilities. DMMPO is responsible for the development of policies for the Defense Medical Standardization Program.

h. **Global Patient Movement Integration Center (GPMIC).** The GPMIC is a joint activity that reports directly to the CDRUSTRANSCOM, the DOD's single manager for the development of policy and standardization of procedures and information support systems for global PM. The GPMIC shall implement policy, and standardization for the regulation, clinical standards, and safe movement of uniformed services and other authorized, or designated patients. The GPMIC orchestrates, and maintains oversight of the theater patient movement requirements centers (TPMRCs) in coordination with the geographic CCMDs and external IGOs as required. The GPMIC is also responsible for the synchronization of current and future operational PM plans to identify available assets and validate transport to bed plans. GPMIC authorizes transfers to medical treatment facilities of the Military Departments of the Department of Veterans Affairs and coordinates global PM requirements with the CCMDs.

i. **Armed Services Blood Program (ASBP).** The ASBP consists of approximately 72 blood banks and blood donor centers worldwide, including 23 Food and Drug Administration licensed blood donor centers. The ASBP plays a key role in providing quality blood products for Service members and their families in both peace and war. As a joint operation among the military Services (Army, Navy, and Air Force), the ASBP has many components working together to collect, process, store, distribute, and transfuse the blood worldwide. The ASBP coordinates with the supported CCDR and USTRANSCOM to ensure blood products distribution meets operational needs.

For additional information concerning the DMMPO, GPMIC, and ASBP, refer to JP 4-02, Health Services.

3. Operational-Level Joint Logistics Staff Organizations

Operational level joint logisticians must provide advice and recommendations to the supported CCDR concerning prioritizations, allocations, or procedural changes based upon the constantly changing operational environment. These boards, centers, cells, and other organizations are defined in terms of roles, responsibilities, locations, and relationships in planning or execution documents.

a. **JLOC.** The JLOC may be established at the CCMD or joint subordinate commands at the discretion of the JFC and operated by the logistics staff. The JLOC is tailored to the mission or operation to coordinate and synchronize the planning and the logistics operations for such functions as engineering, OCS, materiel readiness, MA, HNS, and other services; and must coordinate closely with the CCMD JDDOC concerning transportation and distribution of supplies.

b. **JDDOC.** JDDOC is a CCMD movement control organization designed to synchronize and optimize national and theater multimodal resources for deployment, distribution, and sustainment. The JDDOC is an integrated operations and fusion center (movement control organization), acting in consonance with the GCC's overall requirements and priorities, and on behalf of the GCC, may direct common user and intratheater distribution operations. The JDDOC is a standing operations center, normally under the direction of the GCC's J-4, but may be placed under other command or staff organizations. The JDDOC may move to a forward-deployed location, or be collocated with a subordinate logistics command, unit, or task force. Regardless of location, the JDDOC retains its direct organizational relationship to the CCMD and does not become a subordinate activity of the host organization to which it may be attached. The JDDOC relies on liaison and collaboration to achieve reach back to access national support capabilities.

For additional information concerning a JDDOC, refer to JP 3-35, Deployment and Redeployment Operations, *and JP 4-09,* Distribution Operations.

c. **Combatant Commander Logistic Procurement Support Board (CLPSB).** The CLPSB is a standing AOR-wide board used to develop OCS policies and procedures; coordinate with other IGOs, NGOs, and HNs on OCS issues and actions; determine the theater support contracting organizational structure; and coordinate with DOD and Military Departments on potential loss of contract support and risk management. This board is normally chaired by a GCC's J-4 representative and includes representatives from each Service component command, DOD CSAs, as well as other government departments and agencies or organizations, concerned with OCS matters.

d. **Joint Requirements Review Board (JRRB).** A JRRB approves and prioritizes JFC-designated, joint logistics-related, high value or high-visibility requirements and determines the proper source of support for those requirements and is normally chaired by the subordinate JFC (either subunified command or JTF-level) deputy commander or J-3. The JRRB is utilized to coordinate and control the requirements generation and prioritization of joint logistics supplies and services that are needed in support of the operational mission. The JRRB is normally made up of representatives of the Service component logistics staffs, SOF component staff, DLA, DCMA, joint staff engineer, communications system directorate of a joint staff, joint staff comptroller, staff judge advocate (SJA), and other JFC staff members as directed. The JRRB should include representatives from the joint contracting support board (JCSB) that have designated theater support and external support contracting organizations. The theater support and external support contracting member's main role in the JRRB process is to inform the other JRRB members which contracting mechanisms are readily available for their particular acquisition to include limits of the local vendor base for each type of support.

e. **JCSB.** The JCSB is established to coordinate and deconflict selected major contracting actions between and within the operational area. The JCSB is also the forum for theater support, Service civil augmentation programs, military construction agent, and other designated in-theater contracting organizations to share information, coordinate acquisition strategies, and to minimize chances of competition and redundancies between individual contracts and/or task orders and look for opportunities to optimize sourcing of similar requirements through common contracts. The JCSB makes recommendations on which specific contracting organizations/contract venues are best suited to fulfill the requirements. The JCSB is normally chaired by the GCC designated Service component or joint theater support contracting command senior contracting official.

f. **Joint Civil-Military Engineering Board (JCMEB).** The CCDR or subordinate JFC may establish a JCMEB to provide overall direction for civil-military construction and engineering requirements in the theater or operational area. The JCMEB is a temporary board; the joint force engineer will provide the secretariat and manage the administrative details of the board. Key members on the board include the J-3 future plans officer, J-4, engineer, CA officer, SJA, and comptroller. Other personnel from the staff, components, DOD agencies or activities in support of the CCMD may also participate.

g. **Joint Environmental Management Board (JEMB).** The CCDR or subordinate JFC may establish a JEMB to assist in managing environmental requirements. The JEMB is a temporary board, chaired by the CCDR or subordinate joint force engineer, with members from the joint force staff, components, and any other required special activities (e.g., legal, medical, and CA). The board establishes policies, procedures, priorities, and the overall direction for environmental management requirements in a JOA. The JEMB will coordinate its activities with the CCMD or subordinate joint force engineering staff.

h. **JFUB.** A JFUB is a joint board that evaluates and reconciles component requests for real estate, use of existing facilities, inter-Service support, and construction to ensure compliance with JFC priorities. The JFC may establish a JFUB to assist in managing Service component use of real estate and existing facilities. The JFUB is a temporary board chaired by the CCMD or subordinate joint force engineer, with members from the joint force staff, components, and any other required special activities (e.g., legal, force protection, comptroller, contracting, and CA). If the JFC decides that all engineer-related decisions will be made at the JCMEB, then the JFUB functions as a working group to forward recommendations for decision to the JCMEB. The JFUB serves as the primary coordination body within the JTF for approving construction projects to support installation and mission requirements.

For additional information concerning a JCMEB, JEMB, and JFUB, refer to JP 3-34, Joint Engineer Operations.

i. **Logistics Coordination Board.** A group formed by the JFC to accomplish broad logistics oversight functions that may include but are not limited to coordinating logistics information, providing logistics guidance, reviewing logistics policies and priorities. The board is normally composed of representatives from the joint force staff, all components, and if required, component subordinate units.

j. **JMC.** The JMC may be established at a subordinate unified or JTF level to coordinate the employment of all means of transportation (including that provided by allies or HNs) to support the CONOPS. This coordination is accomplished through establishment of theater and JTF transportation policies within the assigned operational area, consistent with relative urgency of need, port and terminal capabilities, transportation asset availability, and priorities set by a JFC. The JTF JMC will work closely with the JDDOC.

For additional information concerning a JMC, refer to JP 4-01, The Defense Transportation System.

k. **TPMRC.** Three permanent TPMRCs are located in US Northern Command, US Pacific Command, and US European Command. The permanent TPMRCs manage the validation and regulation of PM within their respective theaters. TPMRCs are responsible for theater-wide PM and coordinate with medical treatment facilities to identify the proper treatment/transportation assets required. The TPMRC communicates the "transport-to-bed" plan to the theater Service transportation component or other agencies responsible for executing the mission. The TPMRC manages the validation and regulation of intratheater) PM within their respective theaters. The TPMRC is responsible for theater-wide PM (e.g., medical regulating and aeromedical evacuation scheduling) and coordinates with theater medical treatment facilities to allocate the proper treatment assets required to support its role. The TPMRC coordinates with other appropriate TPMRCs and the GPMIC to coordinate inter-theater PM.

l. **Joint Patient Movement Requirements Center (JPMRC).** A joint activity established to coordinate the joint patient movement requirements function for a JTF operating within a unified command AOR. The JPMRC coordinates with the permanent TPMRC for intratheater PM and with the TPMRC-America for intertheater PM, as required. Synchronization of plans and additional guidance related to the world wide PM system shall be coordinated through the GPMIC.

m. **Joint Blood Program Office (JBPO).** The JBPO is under the staff supervision of the CCMD surgeon. This office is responsible for the joint blood program management in the theater of operations. The JBPO advises the CCMD surgeon on all matters pertaining to theater blood management activities; and evaluates the JBPO, blood product depots, blood transshipment centers, and blood supply units to ensure that personnel, equipment, and resource requirements are addressed in the GCC's OPLANs.

For additional information concerning a TPMRC, JPMRC, and JBPO, refer to JP 4-02, Health Services.

n. **Joint Petroleum Office (JPO).** The JPO, established by the GCC, works in conjunction with its Service components, SAPOs, and DLA Energy to plan, coordinate, and oversee all phases of bulk petroleum support for US forces employed or planned for possible employment in the AOR. JPOs typically have a mix of Service representatives.

o. **SAPO.** When tactical operations warrant extensive management of wholesale bulk petroleum in a JOA, the GCC's JPO may establish a SAPO. Staff augmentation may be provided by Service components. The primary function of the SAPO is to discharge the staff petroleum logistics responsibilities of the JTF. Through the SAPO, the JFC establishes policies, procedures, priorities, and oversight to optimize critical POL support for the JTF. The SAPO is responsible for POL planning and execution within the JOA. This level of planning focuses on support for each Service component. Its products are the inland petroleum distribution plan and base support plans. The SAPO conforms to the administrative and technical procedures established by the GCC and DLA Energy.

For additional information concerning a JPO or SAPO, refer to JP 4-03, Joint Bulk Petroleum and Water Doctrine.

p. **JMAO.** The GCC will normally establish and operate a JMAO that has responsibility for the development, implementation, and oversight of the MA support plan. The JMAO will maintain data and records on temporary internment and the recovery status of all deceased and missing personnel. The joint MA officer coordinates programs for search, recovery, tentative identification, temporary disposition, and evacuation of human remains and serves as the clearing point for MA information. At the discretion of the GCC, the commander, JTF, may direct a JMAO be established in the JOA. The JTF JMAO is established and organized to plan, coordinate, and execute all MA programs. The JTF J-4 has staff supervision responsibility for the JMAO.

For additional information concerning a JMAO, refer to JP 4-06, Mortuary Affairs.

q. **Explosive Hazards Coordination Cell (EHCC).** The JFC may use an explosives hazards team to establish an EHCC to support the land component commander to predict, track, distribute information on, and mitigate explosive hazards within the theater that affect force application, focused logistics, protection, and awareness of the operational environment. The EHCC should establish and maintain an explosive hazard database, conduct pattern analysis, investigate mine and improvised explosive device strikes on route clearance operations, and track unexploded ordnance hazard areas. The cell provides technical advice on the mitigation of explosive hazards, including the development of tactics, techniques, and procedures, and provides training updates to field route clearance units. The EHCC is responsible for performing munitions risk assessments and providing munitions risk information during the planning process.

For additional information concerning an EHCC, refer to JP 3-34, Joint Engineer Operations, *and JP 3-15.1,* Counter-Improvised Explosive Device Operations.

r. **Joint Munitions Office (JMO).** The JMO, established by the GCC, works in conjunction with the Service components, functional components, and subordinate commands, Service acquisition, force providers, and materiel commands, and USD(AT&L) to plan, coordinate, and oversee all phases of ammunition and ordnance support for forces employed or planned for possible employment in the AOR. JMOs typically have a mix of munitions and logistics planners from each Service and ensure proper reporting of readiness status based upon the Joint Munitions Requirement Process and the CJCS's readiness system. Of particular importance to the GCC's JMO's munitions readiness reporting are joint critical munitions, which are the set of precision guided munitions and other ordnance with limited inventories absolutely essential to prosecuting required targets outlined in the OPLAN phased threat distribution, and for which there are no suitable secondary standard munitions alternatives.

Intentionally Blank

APPENDIX D
LOGISTICS-RELATED EXECUTIVE AGENTS

Figure D-1 lists the EAs for a specific area as designated by the reference listed.

Department of Defense Logistics-Related Executive Agents		
Reference	Subject	Executive Agent
DODD 1300.22E	Mortuary Affairs Policy	SECARMY
DODD 2310.01E	The Department of Defense Detainee Program	SECARMY
DODI 3216.01	Use of Animals in DOD Programs	SECARMY for DOD Veterinary Services Program
DODD 3235.02E	DOD Combat Feeding Research and Engineer Program, DOD Combat Feeding Research and Engineering Board, and DOD Nutrition Committee	SECARMY
DODD 4500.09E	Transportation and Traffic Management	CDRUSTRANSCOM for Customs and Border Clearance Program SECARMY for the Military Assistance to Safety and Traffic Program
DODD 4705.1	Management of Land-Based Water Resources in Support of Contingency Operations	SECARMY
DODD 5101.8	DOD Executive Agent for Bulk Petroleum	Dir DLA
DODD 5101.9	DOD Executive Agent for Medical Materiel	Dir DLA
DODD 5101.10	DOD Executive Agent for Subsistence	Dir DLA
DODD 5101.11E	DOD Executive Agent for the Military Postal Service (MPS) and Official Mail Program (OMP)	SECARMY
DODD 5101.12	DOD Executive Agent for Construction/Barrier Materiel	Dir DLA
DODD 5101.13E	DOD Executive Agent for the Unexploded Ordnance Center of Excellence (UXOCOE)	SECARMY
DODD 5154.24	Armed Force Institute of Pathology	SECARMY
DODD 5154.25E	DOD Medical Examination Review Board (MERB)	SECAF
DODD 6000.12E	Health Service Support	SECARMY for ASBP Office
DODD 6055.9E	Explosives Safety Management and the DOD Explosives Safety Board	SECARMY for DOD emergency response to transportation mishaps involving DOD munitions

Figure D-1. Department of Defense Logistics-Related Executive Agents

Department of Defense Logistics-Related Executive Agents (Cont'd)		
DODI 6205.4	Immunization of Other Than US Forces for Biological Warfare Defense	SECARMY for the Immunization Program
DODD 6400.4	DOD Veterinary Services Program	SECARMY
DODD 6490.02E	Comprehensive Health Surveillance	SECARMY for the Defense Armed Forces Health Surveillance Center (AFHSC)
CJCSI 6723.01B	Global Combat Support Family Of Systems Requirements Management And Governance Structure	Director, Joint Staff
DODD 8190.1	DOD Logistics Use of Electronic Data Interchange (EDI) Standards	Director, DLA
https://dod-executiveagent.whs.mil/index.cfm		
Legend ASBP Armed Services Blood Program CDRUSTRANSCOM Commander, United States Transportation Command CJCSI Chairman of the Joint Chiefs of Staff instruction Dir DLA Director, Defense Logistics Agency DOD Department of Defense DODD Department of Defense directive DODI Department of Defense instruction SECAF Secretary of the Air Force SECARMY Secretary of the Army		

Figure D-1. Department of Defense Logistics-Related Executive Agents (Cont'd)

APPENDIX E
GEOGRAPHIC COMBATANT COMMANDER LOGISTICS CONTROL FACTORS AND TOOLS AVAILABLE

1. General

This appendix provides amplifying information detailing the joint logistics factors and enablers with regard to the staff and organization control options.

2. Factors to Establish Logistics Control within the Joint Logistics Environment

GCCs require visibility over the JLEnt to meet the command priorities. The factors below should be considered when the GCC is establishing the logistics control required by the JFC. These factors are not absolute nor all inclusive; but they do reflect the best practices observed in the field. These factors are applicable regardless of the control option selected by the GCC.

a. **Centralized Joint Logistics Planning.** This factor implies a capability to match joint logistics planning with the planning done during the execution of a mission.

b. **Maintenance of Situational Awareness.** This factor represents more than using radio signals and internet-based application data to track cargo movement (ITV). It involves elements such as the design and use of logistics situation reports and the building of ground truth in logistics input to the JFC's COP.

c. **Adjudication of Conflicting Priorities.** This factor is to have processes in place to identify conflicts when following the commander's priorities. For example, a reliable logistics input to the JFC's COP may provide the means to identify conflicts, and a fusion cell may provide the capability to adjudicate.

d. **Timely Identification of Factors and Shortfalls.** To meet this factor a process that links the logistics portion of the battle rhythm with the planning windows must exist.

e. **Clear Understanding of Component Capabilities.** This factor involves the building of databases that reflect current Service component and support agencies logistics capabilities. Fulfilling this factor may require liaison and physical presence of logisticians representing all appropriate Service components within the selected joint logistics control option.

f. **Ability to Synchronize Components Capabilities.** This factor matches the best capability, regardless of Service component, to the joint logistics need.

g. **Integrated Logistics Processes.** This factor is founded on the notion that the joint logistic staff comprehends the Service components logistic processes and uses this understanding to build the visibility required by the JFC to control joint logistics.

h. **Integrated Distribution.** This factor deals with the establishment of the JDDOC and its integration within the joint theater logistics construct. It maximizes the capabilities of the JDDOC to fill the seams between strategic and operational level deployment and distribution tasks. The JDDOC also strives to maximize and synchronize the use of common user land transportation and intratheater lift.

i. **Coordinated Component Supply.** This factor involves the establishment of CUL responsibilities and the processes required to achieve their execution.

j. **Cross Component AV.** This factor refers to the ability for the Service components to see and understand assets available from other components.

k. **Improved Capability to Direct the Process.** This factor proposes the establishment of a decision-making process to direct logistics actions. These actions usually are directed in the form of further guidance to enhance the planning or assessment processes, or the publication of a FRAGORD to direct an action.

3. Tools Available to Enable Joint Logistics Control

The tools described in this paragraph represent those that have proven effective at providing a capability to control joint logistics. The tools apply regardless of the option selected by the commander to control joint logistics.

a. **Logistics Input to the JFC's COP.** This provides dynamic, shareable, real-time actionable information, tailored to meet the commander's requirements. This includes the logistic information required by joint logisticians and operators. It is the tool through which GCCs and subordinate commanders can visualize the logistic environment in their operational area. It supports staff and command activities within the organization and enables users to participate in and support activities external to the command.

(1) All components and supporting agencies in the joint force should have the ability to post and access common sets of information. Additionally, planners and decision makers can tailor information displays respective to their needs. The tailored standardized posting and retrieval processes, and the displays generated from this common source of information in a virtual repository, provide enhanced shared operational environment awareness.

(2) Logisticians access informational links to a virtual library—where OPLANs, OPORDs, FRAGORDs, doctrine, instructions, and policies reside. In addition, links to the CCDR's COP and other significant organizations enhance the ability of logisticians to perform their tasks. Externally, the logistics input to the JFC's COP supports the planning process with links to collaboration sites, such as video-teleconferencing and virtual meeting rooms, allowing real-time information sharing.

b. **Logistics Standard Operating Procedures (SOPs).** The logistics SOP focuses on theater operational level joint logistics and contains procedures to execute joint logistics.

APPENDIX F
CONTINGENCY BASING

1. Introduction

The joint force must be capable of projecting and sustaining power globally. The establishment of contingency basing in support of operations is a fundamental requirement to sustain joint forces. A theater contingency basing strategy translates strategic objectives into a physical presence in a theater. This appendix demonstrates how to effectively and efficiently support operations without overly burdening leaders and operational elements. The accompanying matrix (see Figure F-1) frames how commanders from theater to company level can plan, design, construct, operate, and close contingency bases in an operational area. This matrix also integrates contingency basing and locations across the array of facilities that may be required in an operational area across a full life cycle at the operational level. This appendix and matrix identifies the key players, responsibilities, and functions for how contingency basing supports those operations.

2. General

GCCs require locations to project forces to accomplish given missions. These locations or bases help extend and maintain operational reach and are vital in projecting and sustaining joint forces. Some bases may exist at the onset of an operation, but typically bases are established when needed to accomplish a specific mission or a variety of missions. Contingency basing is the life-cycle process of planning, designing, constructing, operating, managing, and transitioning or closing a non-enduring location supporting a GCC's requirements. Contingency locations are non-enduring locations that support and sustain operations during named or unnamed contingencies or other operations as directed by appropriate authority and are categorized by mission life-cycle requirements as initial, temporary, or semi-permanent. Contingency locations currently have many labels, e.g., forward operating bases, patrol bases, combat outposts, and intermediate staging bases, but all are a combination of the mission and the underlying concept—the base. Contingency locations are essential to support and sustain joint forces across the full range of military operations. They are developed to support joint, interagency, intergovernmental, and multinational partners as per CCDR requirements until successful mission accomplishment. When viewed from a contingency location perspective, this capability is known as BOS: the personnel, equipment, services, activities, and resources required to sustain operations at an installation. The life-cycle attributes of a contingency location are: mission, construction standards, population size, physical size, and level of services. Actions pertaining to the contingency location life-cycle are handled at every echelon from policy decisions at the joint level down to execution tasks conducted by Service and SOF units.

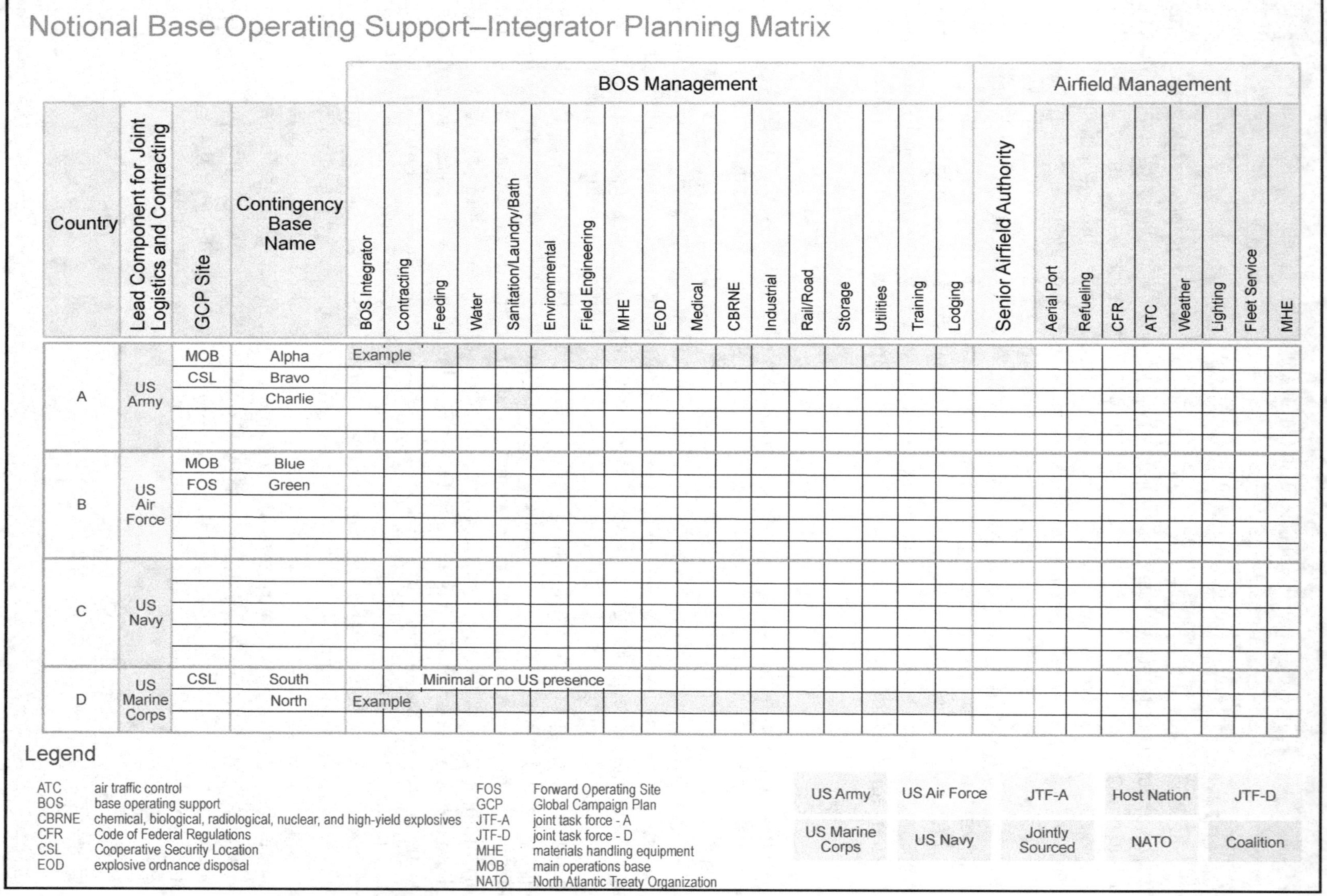

Figure F-1. Notional Base Operating Support–Integrator Planning Matrix

3. Basing Life Cycle

The basic life cycle of a contingency location is planning, designing, constructing, operating, managing, and transitioning or closing. The GCC designates a Service component commander to lead the development of a base required to perform a mission as required by the CONOPS. The Services each have capabilities they employ to accomplish the phases listed below:

a. **Planning.** The planning phase involves the specific tasks conducted to gather, generate, and share the information needed to establish a contingency location capable of supporting the mission objectives of the unit(s) intended to beddown at the location for a planned longevity.

b. **Design.** The design phase correlates construction standards and operational limitations against the location's requirements to create the engineering and construction products needed for the facilities and infrastructure that comprise the entire contingency location.

c. **Construction.** The construction phase applies the horizontal and vertical construction capabilities to the planning products to build, modify, and/or upgrade, as required, the facilities and infrastructure that comprise the entire contingency location.

See JP 3-34, Joint Engineering Operations, *for additional information on these phases.*

d. **Operations.** The operations phase is the execution of C2 over the numerous support and service functional areas that comprise BOS.

e. **Management.** The management phase enforces the process standards for the numerous functional areas that provide the BOS at the desired level(s) of service.

f. **Transition or Closure.** This final phase is a determination on the disposition of a contingency location as driven by mission requirements. If the location is still required but the mission has changed, it might be transitioned to a new lead agent or it might be redesignated as an enduring location under the US Global Defense Posture process. If the location is no longer needed the base may be closed.

4. Levels of Services

The levels of capabilities describe the characteristics of a contingency location in terms of logistic and personnel services, construction standards, and mission support commensurate with the anticipated mission longevity. The net result of these capabilities is an overall quality of life for the base personnel. Short-duration missions are typically more austere, thus lower quality of life by design, while longer-duration missions generally require more resources and result in a higher quality of life.

a. **Personnel Services.** In addition to the logistic services described in Chapter II, "Core Logistics Functions," the following personnel services may be provided at temporary and semi-permanent contingency locations:

       (1) Finance

       (2) Postal

       (3) Legal

       (4) Religious

       (5) Morale, welfare, and recreation

       (6) Base/post exchange

   b. **Infrastructure Services.** Infrastructure services are also vital to contingency location operations. These services provide the 'backbone' of a location. They are:

       (1) Emergency (Fire and Medical)

       (2) General engineering

       (3) Protection

       (4) Communications

       (5) Base support vehicles

       (6) Airfield management (if an airbase)

       (7) Port (if present)

APPENDIX G
REFERENCES

The development of JP 4-0, *Joint Logistics,* is based upon the following primary references:

1. **Federal Law**

    a. *Title 10, USC.*

    b. *Title 14, USC.*

    c. *Title 32, USC.*

2. **Strategic Guidance and Policy**

    a. *The National Defense Strategy.*

    b. *The National Military Strategy.*

    c. *The National Security Strategy.*

    d. *National Response Framework.*

    e. *The National Strategy for Homeland Security.*

    f. *Unified Command Plan.*

    g. *Guidance for Employment of the Force.*

3. **Department of Defense Publications**

    a. DOD 4140.1-R, *DOD Supply Chain Materiel Management Regulation.*

    b. DODD 1300.22E, *Mortuary Affairs Policy.*

    c. DODD 2010.9, *Acquisition and Cross-Servicing Agreements.*

    d. DODD 2310.01E, *The Department of Defense Detainee Program.*

    e. DODD 3000.06, *Combat Support Agencies.*

    f. DODD 3000.10, *Contingency Basing Outside the United States.*

    g. DODD 3235.02E, *DOD Combat Feeding Research and Engineering Board, and DOD Nutrition Committee.*

    h. DODD 4151.18, *Maintenance of Military Materiel.*

i. DODD 4270.5, *Military Construction.*

j. DODD 4500.09E, *Transportation and Traffic Management.*

k. DODD 4705.1, *Management of Land-Based Water Resources in Support of Joint Contingency Operations.*

l. DODD 5100.01, *Functions of the Department of Defense and Its Major Components.*

m. DODD 5101.1, *DOD Executive Agent.*

n. DODD 5101.8, *DOD Executive Agent for Bulk Petroleum.*

o. DODD 5101.9, *DOD Executive Agent for Medical Materiel.*

p. DODD 5101.10, *DOD Executive Agent for Subsistence.*

q. DODD 5101.11E, *DOD Executive Agent for the Military Postal Service (MPS) and Official Mail Program (OMP).*

r. DODD 5101.12, *DOD Executive Agent for Construction/Barrier Materiel.*

s. DODD 5101.13E, *DOD Executive Agent for the Unexploded Ordnance Center of Excellence.*

t. DODD 5111.1, *Under Secretary of Defense for Policy (USD[P]).*

u. DODD 5134.01, *Under Secretary of Defense for Acquisition, Technology, and Logistics (USD[AT&L]).*

v. DODD 5134.12, *Assistant Secretary of Defense for Logistics and Materiel Readiness (ASD[L&MR]).*

w. DODD 5134.15, *Assistant Secretary of Defense for Operational Energy Plans and Programs (ASD[OEPP]).*

x. DODD 5154.24, *Armed Force Institute of Pathology (AFIP).*

y. DODD 5154.25E, *DOD Medical Examination Review Board (MERB).*

z. DODD 5158.04, *United States Transportation Command (USTRANSCOM).*

aa. DODD 5160.65, *Single Manager for Conventional Ammunition (SMCA).*

bb. DODD 6000.12E, *Health Services Support.*

cc. DODD 6055.9E, *Explosives Safety Management and the DOD Explosives Safety Board.*

dd. DODD 6200.04, *Force Health Protection (FHP).*

ee. DODD 6205.3, *DOD Immunization Program for Biological Warfare Defense.*

ff. DODD 6400.4, *DOD Veterinary Services Program.*

gg. DODD 6490.02E, *Comprehensive Health Surveillance.*

hh. DODD 8190.1, *DOD Logistics Use of Electronic Data Interchange (EDI) Standards.*

ii. DODI 1100.22, *Policy and Procedures for Determining Workforce Mix.*

jj. DODI 3110.06, *War Reserve Materiel (WRM) Policy.*

kk. DODI 3216.01, *Use of Animals in DOD Programs.*

ll. DODI 4140.01, *DOD Supply Chain Materiel Management Policy.*

mm. DODI 4140.63, *Management of DOD Clothing and Textiles (Class II).*

nn. DODI 5158.05, *Joint Deployment Process Owner.*

oo. DODI 5158.06, *Distribution Process Owner (DPO).*

pp. DODI 6200.02, *Application of Food and Drug Administration (FDA) Rules to Department of Defense Force Health Protection Programs.*

qq. *Department of Defense Foreign Clearance Guide* (https://www.fcg.pentagon.mil).

4. Chairman of the Joint Chiefs of Staff Publications

a. CJCSI 2120.01B, *Acquisition and Cross-Servicing Agreements.*

b. CJCSI 3110.01, *Joint Strategic Capabilities Plan.*

c. CJCSI 3110.03D, *Logistics Supplement to the Joint Strategic Capabilities Plan (CJCP).*

d. CJCSI 3170.01H, *Joint Capabilities Integration and Development System.*

e. CJCSI 6723.01B, *Global Combat Support Family of Systems Requirements Management and Governance Structure.*

f. CJCSM 3122.01A, *Joint Operation Planning and Execution System (JOPES), Volume I, Planning Policies and Procedures.*

g. CJCSM 3122.02D, *Joint Operation Planning and Execution System (JOPES), Volume III, Time-Phased Force and Deployment Data Development and Deployment Execution.*

h. CJCSM 3130.03, *Adaptive Planning and Execution (APEX) Planning Formats and Guidance.*

i. CJCSM 3150.14B, *Joint Reporting Structure—Logistics.*

j. JP 1, *Doctrine for the Armed Forces of the United States.*

k. JP 1-0, *Joint Personnel Support.*

l. JP 1-02, *Department of Defense Dictionary of Military and Associated Terms.*

m. JP 2-03, *Geospatial Intelligence in Joint Operations.*

n. JP 3-0, *Joint Operations.*

o. JP 3-05, *Special Operations.*

p. JP 3-08, *Interorganizational Coordination During Joint Operations.*

q. JP 3-10, *Joint Security Operations in Theater.*

r. JP 3-11, *Operations in Chemical, Biological, Radiological, and Nuclear Environments.*

s. JP 3-15, *Barriers, Obstacles, and Mine Warfare for Joint Operations.*

t. JP 3-28, *Defense Support of Civil Authorities.*

u. JP 3-29, *Foreign Humanitarian Assistance.*

v. JP 3-33, *Joint Task Force Headquarters.*

w. JP 3-34, *Joint Engineer Operations.*

x. JP 3-35, *Deployment and Redeployment Operations.*

y. JP 3-40, *Countering Weapons of Mass Destruction.*

z. JP 3-41, *Chemical, Biological, Radiological, and Nuclear, Consequence Management.*

aa. JP 3-57, *Civil-Military Operations.*

bb. JP 3-63, *Detainee Operations.*

cc. JP 4-01, *The Defense Transportation System.*

dd. JP 4-02, *Health Services.*

ee. JP 4-03, *Joint Bulk Petroleum and Water Doctrine.*

ff. JP 4-05, *Joint Mobilization Planning.*

gg. JP 4-06, *Mortuary Affairs.*

hh. JP 4-08, *Logistics in Support of Multinational Operations.*

ii. JP 4-09, *Distribution Operations.*

jj. JP 4-10, *Operational Contract Support.*

kk. JP 5-0, *Joint Operation Planning.*

ll. JP 6-0, *Joint Communications System.*

Intentionally Blank

APPENDIX H
ADMINISTRATIVE INSTRUCTIONS

1. User Comments

Users in the field are highly encouraged to submit comments on this publication to: Joint Staff J-7, Deputy Director, Joint Education and Doctrine, ATTN: Joint Doctrine Analysis Division, 116 Lake View Parkway, Suffolk, VA 23435-2697. These comments should address content (accuracy, usefulness, consistency, and organization), writing, and appearance.

2. Authorship

The Director of Logistics (J-4) is the lead agent and Joint Staff doctrine sponsor for this publication.

3. Supersession

This publication supersedes JP 4-0, *Joint Logistic*s, 18 July 2008; and JP 4-07, *Joint Tactics, Techniques, and Procedures for Common-User Logistics During Joint Operations*, 11 June 2001, is cancelled.

4. Change Recommendations

a. Recommendations for urgent changes to this publication should be submitted:

TO: JOINT STAFF WASHINGTON DC//J7-JE&D//

b. Routine changes should be submitted electronically to the Deputy Director, Joint Education and Doctrine, ATTN: Joint Doctrine Analysis Division, and info the lead agent and the Director for Joint Force Development, J-7/JE&D.

c. When a Joint Staff directorate submits a proposal to the CJCS that would change source document information reflected in this publication, that directorate will include a proposed change to this publication as an enclosure to its proposal. The Services and other organizations are requested to notify the Joint Staff J-7 when changes to source documents reflected in this publication are initiated.

5. Distribution of Publications

Local reproduction is authorized, and access to unclassified publications is unrestricted. However, access to and reproduction authorization for classified JPs must be IAW DOD Manual 5200.01, Volume 1, *DOD Information Security Program: Overview, Classification, and Declassification,* and DOD Manual 5200.01, Volume 3, *DOD Information Security Program: Protection of Classified Information.*

6. Distribution of Electronic Publications

a. Joint Staff J-7 will not print copies of JPs for distribution. Electronic versions are available on JDESI at https://jdeis.js.mil (NIPRNET) and http://jdeis.js.smil.mil (SIPRNET), and on the JEL at http://www.dtic.mil/doctrine (NIPRNET).

b. Only approved JPs are releasable outside the CCMDs, Services, and Joint Staff. Release of any classified JP to foreign governments or foreign nationals must be requested through the local embassy (Defense Attaché Office) to DIA, Defense Foreign Liaison/IE-3, 200 MacDill Blvd., Joint Base Anacostia-Bolling, Washington, DC 20340-5100.

c. JEL CD-ROM. Upon request of a joint doctrine development community member, the Joint Staff J-7 will produce and deliver one CD-ROM with current JPs. This JEL CD-ROM will be updated not less than semi-annually and when received can be locally reproduced for use within the CCMDs, Services, and CSAs.

GLOSSARY
PART I—ABBREVIATIONS AND ACRONYMS

A-1	director of manpower, personnel, and services (Air Force)
A-4	director of logistics (Air Force)
A-7	director of installations and mission support (Air Force)
ACSA	acquisition and cross-servicing agreement
AETF	air and space expeditionary task force
AOR	area of responsibility
APEX	Adaptive Planning and Execution
ASBP	Armed Services Blood Program
ASCC	Army Service component command
ASD(L&MR)	Assistant Secretary of Defense for Logistics and Materiel Readiness
ASD(OEPP)	Assistant Secretary of Defense for Operational Energy Plans and Programs
AV	asset visibility
BOS	base operating support
BOS-I	base operating support-integrator
BPC	building partnership capacity
C2	command and control
CCDR	combatant commander
CCIR	commander's critical information requirement
CCMD	combatant command
CDRTSOC	commander, theater special operations command
CDRUSSOCOM	Commander, United States Special Operations Command
CDRUSTRANSCOM	Commander, United States Transportation Command
CJCS	Chairman of the Joint Chiefs of Staff
CJCSI	Chairman of the Joint Chiefs of Staff instruction
CJCSM	Chairman of the Joint Chiefs of Staff manual
CLPSB	combatant commander logistic procurement support board
COA	course of action
COCOM	combatant command (command authority)
COI	community of interest
COLS	concept of logistic support
COMAFFOR	commander, Air Force forces
CONOPS	concept of operations
CONPLAN	concept plan
COP	common operational picture
CS	combat support
CSA	combat support agency
CSS	combat service support
CUL	common-user logistics

DAFL	directive authority for logistics
DCMA	Defense Contract Management Agency
DDOC	Deployment and Distribution Operations Center (USTRANSCOM)
DHB	Defense Health Board
DLA	Defense Logistics Agency
DMMPO	Defense Medical Materiel Program Office
DOD	Department of Defense
DODD	Department of Defense directive
DODI	Department of Defense instruction
DPO	distribution process owner
DSCA	Defense Security Cooperation Agency
EA	executive agent
EHCC	explosive hazards coordination cell
ESC	expeditionary sustainment command
FHP	force health protection
FRAGORD	fragmentary order
GCC	geographic combatant commander
GCSS-J	Global Combat Support System-Joint
GEF	Guidance for Employment of the Force
GPMIC	Global Patient Movement Integration Center
HN	host nation
HS	health services
HSD	health service delivery
IGO	intergovernmental organization
IPR	in-progress review
ITV	in-transit visibility
J-3	operations directorate of a joint staff
J-4	logistics directorate of a joint staff
J-5	plans directorate of a joint staff
JBPO	joint blood program office
JCMEB	joint civil-military engineer board
JCSB	joint contracting support board
JDDE	joint deployment and distribution enterprise
JDDOC	joint deployment and distribution operations center
JDPO	joint deployment process owner
JEMB	joint environmental management board
JFC	joint force commander
JFUB	joint facilities utilization board
JLEnt	joint logistics enterprise
JLOC	joint logistics operations center

JMAO	joint mortuary affairs office
JMC	joint movement center
JMO	joint munitions office
JMPAB	Joint Materiel Priorities and Allocation Board
JOA	joint operations area
JOPES	Joint Operation Planning and Execution System
JOPP	joint operation planning process
JP	joint publication
JPMRC	joint patient movement requirements center
JPO	joint petroleum office
JPSE	Joint Planning Support Element (USTRANSCOM)
JRRB	joint requirements review board
JRSOI	joint reception, staging, onward movement and integration
JSCP	Joint Strategic Capabilities Plan
JSOTF	joint special operations task force
JTB	Joint Transportation Board
JTF	joint task force
JTF-PO	joint task force-port opening
LOC	line of communications
LRC	logistics readiness center
LSA	logistics supportability analysis
MA	mortuary affairs
MEF	Marine expeditionary force
MHS	Military Health System
MLG	Marine logistics group
NGO	nongovernmental organization
NIPRNET	Nonsecure Internet Protocol Router Network
OCS	operational contract support
OPCON	operational control
OPLAN	operation plan
OPORD	operation order
PM	patient movement
PN	partner nation
POD	port of debarkation
POL	petroleum, oils, and lubricants
PSA	principal staff assistant
SAA	senior airfield authority
SAPO	subarea petroleum office
SecDef	Secretary of Defense
SG	surgeon general

SIPRNET	SECRET Internet Protocol Router Network
SITREP	situation report
SJA	staff judge advocate
SOF	special operations forces
SOP	standard operating procedure
TCP	theater campaign plan
TLA	theater logistics analysis
TLO	theater logistics overview
TPFDD	time-phased force and deployment data
TPMRC	theater patient movement requirements center
TSC	theater sustainment command (Army)
TSOC	theater special operations command
USC	United States Code
USD(AT&L)	Under Secretary of Defense for Acquisition, Technology, and Logistics
USD(P)	Under Secretary of Defense for Policy
USSOCOM	United States Special Operations Command
USTRANSCOM	United States Transportation Command

PART II—TERMS AND DEFINITIONS

base. 1. A locality from which operations are projected or supported. 2. An area or locality containing installations which provide logistics or other support. 3. Home airfield or home carrier. (JP 1-02. SOURCE: JP 4-0)

base operating support. Directly assisting, maintaining, supplying, and distributing support of forces at the operating location. (Also called **BOS.**) (Approved for inclusion in JP 1-02.)

base operating support-integrator. The designated Service component or joint task force commander assigned to synchronize all sustainment functions for a contingency base. Also called **BOS-I.** (Approved for inclusion in JP 1-02.)

combat service support. The essential capabilities, functions, activities, and tasks necessary to sustain all elements of all operating forces in theater at all levels of war. Also called **CSS.** (Approved for incorporation in JP 1-02.)

combat support. Fire support and operational assistance provided to combat elements. Also called **CS.** (JP 1-02. SOURCE: JP 4-0)

common-user item. An item of an interchangeable nature that is in common use by two or more nations or Services of a nation. (Approved for incorporation into JP 1-02.)

component. 1. One of the subordinate organizations that constitute a joint force. (JP 1) 2. In logistics, a part or combination of parts having a specific function, which can be installed or replaced only as an entity. Also called **COMP.** (JP 1-02. SOURCE: JP 4-0)

concept of logistic support. A verbal or graphic statement, in a broad outline, of how a commander intends to support and integrate with a concept of operations in an operation or campaign. Also called **COLS.** (Approved for incorporation into JP 1-02.)

consumer logistics. None. (Approved for removal from JP 1-02.)

contingency retention stock. None. (Approved for removal from JP 1-02.)

critical supplies and materiel. None. (Approved for removal from JP 1-02.)

cross-leveling. At the theater strategic and operational levels, it is the process of diverting en route or in-theater materiel from one military element to meet the higher priority of another within the combatant commander's directive authority for logistics. (Approved for incorporation into JP 1-02.)

depot. 1. supply—An activity for the receipt, classification, storage, accounting, issue, maintenance, procurement, manufacture, assembly, research, salvage, or disposal of material. 2. personnel—An activity for the reception, processing, training, assignment, and forwarding of personnel replacements. (JP 1-02. SOURCE: JP 4-0)

depot maintenance. None. (Approved for removal from JP 1-02.)

distribution. 1. The arrangement of troops for any purpose, such as a battle, march, or maneuver. 2. A planned pattern of projectiles about a point. 3. A planned spread of fire to cover a desired frontage or depth. 4. An official delivery of anything, such as orders or supplies. 5. The operational process of synchronizing all elements of the logistic system to deliver the "right things" to the "right place" at the "right time" to support the geographic combatant commander. 6. The process of assigning military personnel to activities, units, or billets. (JP 1-02. SOURCE: JP 4-0)

dominant user. The Service or multinational partner who is the principal consumer of a particular common-user logistic supply or service within a joint or multinational operation and will normally act as the lead Service to provide this particular common-user logistic supply or service to other Service components, multinational partners, other governmental agencies, or nongovernmental agencies as directed by the combatant commander. (Approved for incorporation into JP 1-02.)

equipment. In logistics, all nonexpendable items needed to outfit or equip an individual or organization. (JP 1-02. SOURCE: JP 4-0)

federal supply class management. None. (Approved for removal from JP 1-02.)

Global Combat Support System-Joint. The primary information technology application used to provide automation support to the joint logistician. Also called **GCSS-J.** (JP 1-02. SOURCE: JP 4-0)

host-nation support. Civil and/or military assistance rendered by a nation to foreign forces within its territory during peacetime, crises or emergencies, or war based on agreements mutually concluded between nations. Also called **HNS.** (JP 1-02. SOURCE: JP 4-0)

hygiene services. The provision of personal hygiene facilities and waste collection; and the cleaning, repair, replacement, and return of individual clothing and equipment items in a deployed environment. (Approved for inclusion in JP 1-02.)

integrated materiel management. None. (Approved for inclusion in JP 1-02.)

inter-Service, intragovernmental agreements. None. (Approved for removal from JP 1-02.)

inter-Service support. Action by one Service or element thereof to provide logistics and/or administrative support to another Service or element thereof. (Approved for incorporation into JP 1-02.)

joint deployment and distribution enterprise. The complex of equipment, procedures, doctrine, leaders, technical connectivity, information, shared knowledge, organizations, facilities, training, and materiel necessary to conduct joint distribution operations. Also called **JDDE.** (Approved for replacement of "Joint Deployment and Distribution Enterprise" in JP 1-02.)

joint logistics. The coordinated use, synchronization, and sharing of two or more Military Departments' logistic resources to support the joint force. (JP 1-02. SOURCE: JP 4-0)

joint logistics enterprise. A multi-tiered matrix of key global logistics providers cooperatively engaged or structured to achieve a common purpose without jeopardizing the integrity of their own organizational missions and goals. Also called **JLEnt.** (Approved for inclusion in JP 1-02.)

joint movement center. None (Approved for removal from JP 1-02.)

lead Service or agency for common-user logistics. A Service component or Department of Defense agency that is responsible for execution of common-user item or service support in a specific combatant command or multinational operation as defined in the combatant or subordinate joint force commander's operation plan, operation order, and/or directives. (Approved for incorporation into JP 1-02 with JP 4-0 as the source JP.)

logistics. Planning and executing the movement and support of forces. (Approved for incorporation into JP 1-02.)

logistics supportability analysis. Combatant command internal assessment for the Joint Strategic Capabilities Plan on capabilities and shortfalls of key logistic capabilities required to execute and sustain the concept of support conducted on all level three plans with the time phased force deployment data. Also called **LSA.** (Approved for inclusion in JP 1-02.)

logistic support. Support that encompasses the logistic services, materiel, and transportation required to support the continental United States-based and worldwide deployed forces. (JP 1-02. SOURCE: JP 4-0)

maintenance. 1. All action, including inspection, testing, servicing, classification as to serviceability, repair, rebuilding, and reclamation, taken to retain materiel in a serviceable condition or to restore it to serviceability. 2. All supply and repair action taken to keep a force in condition to carry out its mission. 3. The routine recurring work required to keep a facility in such condition that it may be continuously used at its original or designed capacity and efficiency for its intended purpose. (Approved for replacement of "maintenance (materiel)" and its definition in JP 1-02.)

maintenance status. None. (Approved for removal from JP 1-02.)

materiel. All items necessary to equip, operate, maintain, and support military activities without distinction as to its application for administrative or combat purposes. (Approval for incorporation into JP 1-02.)

most capable Service or agency. None. (Approved for removal from JP 1-02.)

operational energy. The energy required for training, moving, and sustaining military forces and weapons platforms for military operations. (Approved for inclusion in JP 1-02.)

organizational equipment. None. (Approved for removal from JP 1-02.)

P-day. None. (Approved for removal from JP 1-02.)

port of debarkation. The geographic point at which cargo or personnel are discharged. Also called **POD.** (Approved for incorporation into JP 1-02.)

pre-position. To place military units, equipment, or supplies at or near the point of planned use or at a designated location to reduce reaction time, and to ensure timely support of a specific force during initial phases of an operation. (JP 1-02. SOURCE: JP 4-0)

process owner. The head of a Department of Defense component assigned a responsibility by the Secretary of Defense when process improvement involves more than one Service or Department of Defense component. (Approved for incorporation into JP 1-02.)

rapid and precise response. None. (Approved for removal from JP 1-02.)

repair. None. (Approved for removal from JP 1-02.)

reset. A set of actions to restore equipment to a desired level of combat capability commensurate with a unit's future mission. (Approved for inclusion in JP 1-02.)

salvage. 1. Property that has some value in excess of its basic material content but is in such condition that it has no reasonable prospect of use for any purpose as a unit and its repair or rehabilitation for use as a unit is clearly impractical. 2. The saving or rescuing of condemned, discarded, or abandoned property, and of materials contained therein for reuse, refabrication, or scrapping. (Approved for incorporation into JP 1-02 with JP 4-0 as the source JP.)

salvage operation. None. (Approved for removal from JP 1-02.)

service ammunition. None. (Approved for removal from JP 1-02.)

servicing. None. (Approved for removal from JP 1-02.)

short supply. None. (Approved for removal from JP 1-02.)

single integrated theater logistic manager. None. (Approved for removal from JP 1-02.)

slice. None. (Approved for removal from JP 1-02.)

supplies. In logistics, all materiel and items used in the equipment, support, and maintenance of military forces. (JP 1-02. SOURCE: JP 4-0)

supply. The procurement, distribution, maintenance while in storage, and salvage of supplies, including the determination of kind and quantity of supplies. a. producer phase—That phase of military supply that extends from determination of procurement schedules to acceptance of finished supplies by the Services. b. consumer phase—That phase of military supply that extends from receipt of finished supplies by the Services through issue for use or consumption. (Approved for incorporation into JP 1-02.)

support items. None. (Approved for removal from JP 1-02.)

Intentionally Blank

JOINT DOCTRINE PUBLICATIONS HIERARCHY

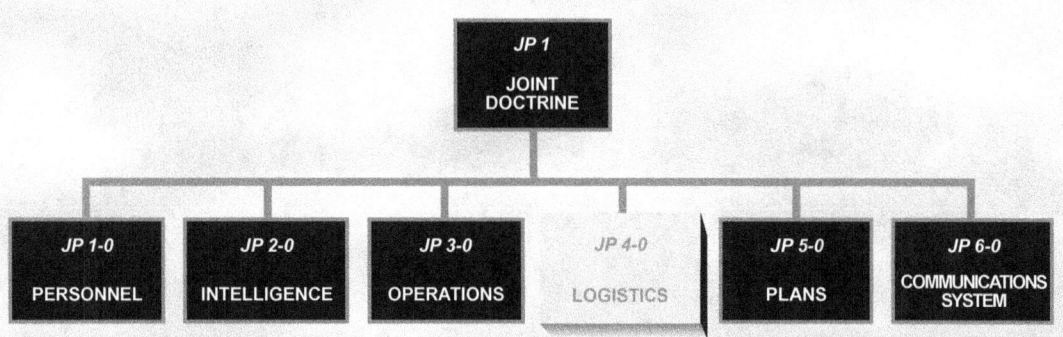

All joint publications are organized into a comprehensive hierarchy as shown in the chart above. **Joint Publication (JP) 4-0** is in the **Logistics** series of joint doctrine publications. The diagram below illustrates an overview of the development process:

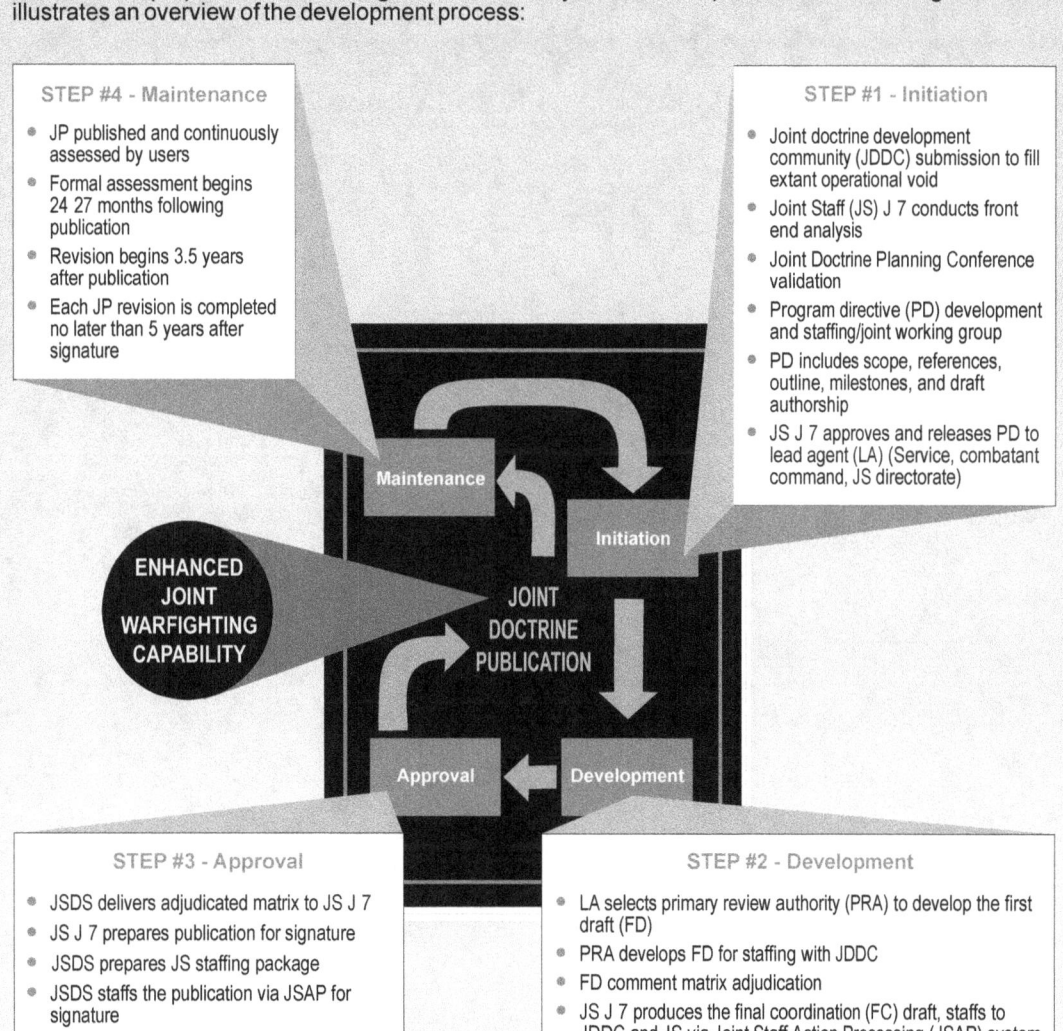

STEP #4 - Maintenance

- JP published and continuously assessed by users
- Formal assessment begins 24 27 months following publication
- Revision begins 3.5 years after publication
- Each JP revision is completed no later than 5 years after signature

STEP #1 - Initiation

- Joint doctrine development community (JDDC) submission to fill extant operational void
- Joint Staff (JS) J 7 conducts front end analysis
- Joint Doctrine Planning Conference validation
- Program directive (PD) development and staffing/joint working group
- PD includes scope, references, outline, milestones, and draft authorship
- JS J 7 approves and releases PD to lead agent (LA) (Service, combatant command, JS directorate)

STEP #3 - Approval

- JSDS delivers adjudicated matrix to JS J 7
- JS J 7 prepares publication for signature
- JSDS prepares JS staffing package
- JSDS staffs the publication via JSAP for signature

STEP #2 - Development

- LA selects primary review authority (PRA) to develop the first draft (FD)
- PRA develops FD for staffing with JDDC
- FD comment matrix adjudication
- JS J 7 produces the final coordination (FC) draft, staffs to JDDC and JS via Joint Staff Action Processing (JSAP) system
- Joint Staff doctrine sponsor (JSDS) adjudicates FC comment matrix
- FC joint working group